Aretha Franklin, Lady Soul

Aretha Franklin, Lady Soul

by Leslie Gourse

AN IMPACT BIOGRAPHY

Franklin Watts
New York / Chicago / London / Toronto / Sydney

In Memory of S. Norman Gourse
and special thanks to my editor E. Russell Primm III

The author and publisher gratefully acknowledge the following for permission
to use copyrighted material:

"Evil Gal Blues," Leonard Feather/Model Music Company (ASCAP). "Respect,"
© 1969 Irving Music Inc. All Rights Reserved. International © Secured. *Where
I'm Coming From*, copyright © Barbara Brandson. Distributed by Universal
Press Syndicate. Reprinted with permission. All rights reserved. *Aretha Franklin:
The Queen of Soul*, by Mark Bego. St. Martin's Press, Inc., New York, N.Y.
copyright © 1989 by Mark Bego. Copyright © 1967/68/70/78/88/
90/91/93 by The New York Times Company. Reprinted by permission.
James T. Jones IV, "Soul of the Queen," *Vanity Fair*, March 1994. Used with
permission from the *Amsterdam News*. "Poem For Aretha," © 1971 Nikki
Giovanni. By permission of the author. © Reprinted by permission of the *New
York Post*. © 1968 Time, Inc. Reprinted by permission. Jerry Wexler and
David Ritz, *Rhythm and the Blues*, New York: Alfred A. Knopf, Inc., ©1993
and used by permission of the authors.

Photographs copyright ©: Frank Driggs Collection: pp. 8, 21 (Popsie
Randolph), 39, 41, 74 (Popsie Randolph), 121; Wide World Photos: pp.
11, 23, 99, 102, 106, 130, 138; Michael Ochs Archives: pp. 26, 30,
32, 36, 46, 55, 57, 64, 92; UPI/Bettmann: pp. 51, 116; Archive Photos:
pp. 77 (DPA), 89, 108, 141 (Fotos International); The Bettmann Archive: p.
97; Retna Ltd./John Bellissimo: p. 113.

Library of Congress Cataloging-in-Publication Data

Gourse, Leslie.
Aretha Franklin : Lady Soul / by Leslie Gourse.
p. cm.—(An Impact biography)
Includes discography and videography.
Includes bibliographical references and index.
ISBN 0-531-13037-1 (lib. bdg.)—ISBN 0-531-15750-4 (pbk.)
1. Franklin, Aretha—Juvenile literature. 2. Soul musicians—
United States—Biography. [1. Franklin, Aretha. 2. Singers.
3. Soul music. 4. Afro-Americans—Biography. 5. Women—Biography.]
I. Title. II. Series.
ML3930.F68G7 1995
782.42164'4'092—dc20
[B] 94-29074   CIP   AC MN

CONTENTS

ONE

A Child of the Revolutionary Sixties

Many of the greatest African-American blues, jazz, pop, and opera singers in the United States first sang gospel music in the churches. On Sundays in church, they sang nearly all day to give themselves courage and spiritual refreshment. Outside of church, most African-Americans lived under cruel and unfair laws enforcing racial prejudice and segregation, simply because of the color of their skin. They were not forbidden, however, to sing and play music in churches. So they developed and nurtured the gospel as a means of spiritual survival.

Their singing was beautiful, with improvised melodies and offbeat rhythms. They became famous in the country for their musical genius, particularly for their singing and organ music in the Baptist churches. In the South, white people, who began enforcing separation of the races with segregation laws around the turn of the twentieth century, used to sit in their cars outside the Baptist churches and listen to the people sing, play organ, piano, and other instruments in the Sanctified, or Pentacostal, churches. Many African-Americans who would become famous in the entertainment world launched their musical careers in churches.

Aretha began her career singing gospel music in a
church choir much like this one in Newark, New Jersey.

Gospel music gave birth to the blues—music that sounded very much like religious hymns. But blues singers used words that expressed the joys and sorrows of their daily lives. The blues could be about love, or money, or betrayal by friends, or poverty—anything at all that could happen in a person's life or imagination. And the blues used the rhythms of gospel music—sometimes slow and steady, or driving and syncopated.

One of the greatest singers to come out of the Baptist gospel tradition is Aretha Franklin. In the 1960s, she became a star by singing both gospel and the blues with a powerful, emotion-fraught voice. She sang with the greatest creativity because her superior understanding of harmonies allowed her to invent elaborate and unique melodies. Like all great gospel, blues, and jazz singers, Aretha saw no sense in going straight from one note to another. Instead she glided around within the music, singing halftones, quarter tones, and microtones. Musicians say that the notes she could sing fall between the cracks—in the spaces between the piano keys. She made spectacular leaps between notes far apart in the scales. Her runs and trills were lightning-fast.

Her emotional outpourings in gospel hymns expressed a profound trust in the Lord and a belief that He could save her. As a pop singer, she directed her passion toward expressing a belief in the power of earthy, sexual, emotional love—for better or for worse—between a man and a woman. She would always be able to communicate her deep feeling to audiences, whether she was singing the hymn "Precious Lord," or her worldly song, "Respect," about the love and lust she wanted her man to feel for her. In her song "Think," which she wrote as a warning to a man that he had better think about what he was doing to their relationship, she shouted out the words praising liberty and freedom. Her message transcended the boundaries of male–female relationships. Her sound was so fervent that it became a rallying cry for the civil rights movement of the 1960s. At that time, the entire country was caught up in revolutionary social changes to promote racial integration and equality, equal rights for women, and personal freedoms for everyone. Aretha's voice made her a leader.

* * *

The daughter of a Baptist minister, Aretha grew up hearing gospel music sung by the most talented singers in the Baptist faith. Her father was the Reverend Clarence La Vaughan Franklin, who became a famous and influential pastor at the New Bethel Baptist Church in Detroit during the late 1940s. He befriended the inspirational Baptist minister and civil rights leader Dr. Martin Luther King, Jr. Legend says that when Dr. King needed financial assistance to lead the civil rights movement in the 1960s, he called Aretha's father. Rev. Franklin was a spellbinding preacher. His followers contributed great sums of money to his church's weekly collection plate, and he shared it with Dr. King.

Aretha was born on March 25, 1942, in Memphis, Tennessee, and moved to Detroit with her family by 1948. Her earliest memories include her father's stirring sermons and her mother's gospel singing. Aretha began singing in her father's church when she was a child. Her elder sister, Erma, and her baby sister, Carolyn, three years younger than Aretha, sang in church, too. All the Franklin girls were talented.

In her early teens, Aretha traveled in a bus around the country with her father, sisters, and her elder brother Cecil. Aretha also had a half-brother, Vaughn—her mother's child by a previous marriage—who may have gone along at times in the gospel caravans to other churches. Many churches sent invitations to the gifted Franklin family.

As a minister's daughter, Aretha was encouraged to join in Baptist traditions wholeheartedly. Even when she became a young woman, she had a well-mannered, girlish way of speaking in a soft, breathless voice with a flat,

*Rev. Martin Luther King, Jr., shown here leading
a civil rights action in Albany, Georgia, in July 1962,
was a close friend of Aretha and her father,
Rev. Clarence L. Franklin.*

midwestern accent. But a spirit of mischief and rebellion stirred in her soul from the time she was a little girl.

She would recall for an interviewer how she had started to play piano by accompanying the records of the popular African-American jazz pianist and composer Eddie Heywood when she was about eight or nine. Her father wasn't upset that Aretha loved secular music. Many Baptist ministers—and other Baptist families for that matter—had strict rules. They wouldn't let their children listen to jazz. But Rev. Franklin was happy about Aretha's talent; he decided to encourage her. He socialized with different types of people, and he loved all kinds of music himself. His worldliness made him controversial at times. Some family friends thought that Aretha was his favorite child. Her talent set her apart and gave her certain privileges.

Rev. Franklin hired a piano teacher, who tried to tone down Aretha's exuberant, natural talent with simple exercises. "Too much 'Chopsticks'," was the way Aretha described the boring lessons that were supposed to give her polish.[1] She wanted to explore the piano in her own free-spirited way. "I used to run and hide," Aretha would often recall, whenever she saw the teacher arrive at the family's big yellow brick house with leaded glass windows in Detroit.[2] Eventually the teacher stopped coming because Aretha was never around to take lessons.

She played the piano on her own, listened to the music and conversation of talented musicians who visited her father, and took advice from them. Many were stars in American gospel, blues, jazz, and pop music. She was also inspired by her father's half-sung, half-spoken sermons. He was so powerful a performer in the pulpit that his sermons were recorded and sold nationwide. And Aretha started to blend everything she learned about music into a unique, new style. It would become known as "soul music," the most popular and exciting music in the country in the 1960s.

Soul music was about reality. As *Time* magazine said in its cover story about Aretha in the late 1960s, soul music is a "homely distillation of everybody's portion of pain and joy."[3] Soul music did away with romantic, pretty notions about the way people lived and felt about each other. "The difference between Tin Pan Alley [a term used to describe old-fashioned popular music] and soul is not hard to define," *Time* continued. "A conventional tune-smith might write, 'You're still near, my darling, though we're apart/I'll hold you always in my heart.' The soul singer might put it, 'Baby, since you split the scene the rent's come due/Without you or your money it's hard, yeah, hard to be true.' "[4]

As Aretha was falling in love with playing and singing soul music in the 1950s, the civil rights movement was taking hold in earnest in the country. A band of brilliant and courageous African-American lawyers was fighting legal battles in the courts to end segregation in education. The most famous of those lawyers was Thurgood Marshall, a future U.S. Supreme Court justice. In 1954 Marshall, along with other lawyers in the legal department of the National Association for the Advancement of Colored People (NAACP), won a landmark case before the U.S. Supreme Court, *Brown v. Board of Education*. The court decided that segregation by race in U.S. schools was illegal because it was impossible to have separate but equal education. Aretha was very much aware of the racial turmoil in the country and the slow progress that was being made to achieve racial integration and equal opportunity. The struggle gave her special strength to sing gospel first, and then the blues, in a fiery style.

When she was still a child, she sang her first solo in her father's church. "I stood up on a little chair and sang," she would recall for several interviewers, including Mark Bego, who wrote a book called *Aretha Franklin, The Queen of Soul*.[5] That was a time-honored tradition for talented young African-American singers. A man who became a famous blues singer in New Orleans recalled how he had begun singing gospel music in church when he was six, in 1913. "I had to stand up on one of those big old high benches, because people couldn't see where the voice was coming from. . . . People just clapped their hands and sang. Some of the most melodious things you ever heard, some of the most gorgeous. . .voices came out of the Baptist church. . .that's where I got the idea to go into music later. . .in the Baptist church."[6] Aretha had the same experience. About forty years after her debut, she told a writer from *Vanity Fair* magazine about singing "Jesus Be a Fence": "It was a favorite song."

"It was something to hear a little girl belting it?" asked the writer.

"Yes," she [said]. . ."Four octaves," referring to her amazing vocal range.[7] And then she smiled, dropping her usual pose of formality and reserve. That was how she faced the public in her middle age, and she rarely dropped her guard.

Aretha's first solo in church impressed her father's congregation mightily. Everybody told him how talented she was. When she was fourteen, she made her first gospel recording. By her late teens, she would rebel against her traditional role. She would always say that she loved gospel music, and she never stopped singing it. Friends knew that she respected her father's ministry profoundly. For a professional career, however, she decided to switch to secular music with gospel-based rhythms, harmonies, and melodies. To those elements, she added worldly, sometimes very sexy, lyrics—"the devil's words," as one of her record producers, Jerry Wexler, would describe them.[8] That was how very religious people regarded secular music.

She began by singing American standards for a big, prestigious recording company, Columbia Records, in 1960. At first she emulated the blues, jazz, and pop stars who had come before her. It was not until 1966 that she asserted her own unfettered, earthy, and abandoned style. At that time, she signed a contract with Atlantic Records, a small company whose owners were sensitive to the emotionalism and excitement of African-American gospel and blues. When Aretha signed with that company, many other young people of all races and religions were committing themselves to bringing about radical changes—racial equality and integration, then heralded as "black power" and "black dignity," and the liberation of women from their traditional subservient roles. Young people were demonstrating for the federal government to end the war in Vietnam, too. Atlantic Records freed Aretha to set the pattern, which was called the "groove," for her own songs, and sing her heart out and play piano the way she wanted to. Her loud, soaring voice and style not only expressed her feelings, they also reflected the political and social changes developing in the country. Her voice had the mystique of a flag.

Aretha, in short, unleashed her voice at a time when people were hell-bent on overcoming racial prejudice and extending their personal freedom. Even though audiences couldn't always understand every word she sang, she sounded like the pounding of their excited pulses. In her own way, she was continuing the influence and following in the footsteps of her father, when he turned his attention to encouraging individual accomplishment and civil rights.

Subtlety was out. Forthrightness, self-assertiveness, expressiveness, speeches, demonstrations, even violent confrontations between groups, were in. Against a society she and some of her contemporaries and elders felt was repressive, Aretha channeled rebellion into music. That was how she became the most lauded and influential female singer of "soul" in the 1960s and early 1970s.

In the 1970s, the reign of soul music ended. Aretha was still a fairly young and energetic singer, and she sought a new direction for her high-energy music. To recover from a lull in her career, she switched to a different recording label, Arista. There she sang some new hits—duets, rock and roll, pop, and danceable disco songs, proving that she could adapt to changing times. She also had a small, unforgettable, and soulful role, singing her own song, "Think," in the 1980 movie *The Blues Brothers*. Her Arista album *Who's Zoomin' Who?* with its hit single, "Freeway of Love," became one of her platinum albums, selling more than a million copies in 1985. From the National Association of Recording Arts and Sciences (NARAS), she won fifteen Grammys by 1992, and, in 1994, NARAS acknowledged her legendary musical influence with a Lifetime Achievement Grammy.

She had established herself as such a great artist with a remarkable voice that her style would never be dismissed as out of date. She recorded, made videos, and traveled to perform at leading concert halls and theaters, singing her old hits. They had become anthems emblematic of her stardom and the exciting period in U.S. social history when she had become famous for delivering messages that had never grown cold. She had become known internationally by her first name alone.

A political cartoonist, Barbara Brandon, in the newspaper *New York Live*, on June 20, 1993, summed up Aretha's public status when she depicted two young African-American women speaking on a telephone. One woman was pregnant, and she had discovered that she was going to have a girl. Her girlfriend suggested several names: "Imani. It means faith." The pregnant woman listened. Or "Shafiq. It means compassion." "That's nice, too," said the expectant mother, "but I've settled on a name that represents and commands respect. . .Aretha."

All the while, behind the scenes, Aretha existed on an emotional roller coaster, living the traditional life of a "diva" and surviving hard luck and violent events that would have crushed a weaker spirit. For the *Time* magazine article, a friend said, "Aretha comes alive only when she's singing."[9] Her faith in her abilities kept her going through personal disasters. Her father had helped form her indestructible belief in her destiny. Though she found herself adrift at times, she always rose above her adversities. She reflected in her middle age, "In 1962, I was crowned the Queen of Soul. . . . It's just second nature to me."[10] She was proud that people were still cheering for her performances in the 1990s.

TWO

GROWING UP FAST

From the beginning of her life, there was always something dramatic happening to her. Aretha Louise Franklin, who was born in Memphis, Tennessee, on March 25, 1942, was only two years old when her father, a Baptist minister with a revivalist flavor to his preaching and gospel singing, decided it was time to take his family north. He had been born in Mississippi, where his father had been a sharecropper and a gambler.[1] Now Aretha's father was seeking greener, freer pastures. He preached to people that they could become anything they wanted to. "Your mental attitude has a lot to do with. . .how successful you'll be in your efforts," he said. His message was about the power of positive prayer, thought, and action. A northern pulpit would be the ideal place for him, he decided. So the forceful preacher and his wife, a gospel singer named Barbara Siggers, headed first to Buffalo, New York, and then moved again to Detroit, Michigan.

The Franklins were almost Johnny-come-latelys to the big African-American community already established in Detroit. Thousands of Southerners had migrated to the booming auto industry city, where they had found jobs. Detroit was not a modern model of integration. African-

Americans lived in their own communities. But segregation wasn't as rigidly enforced as it was in the South. In Detroit, Rev. Franklin, a big, strapping man with an outgoing showman's personality, followed the principles for success that he preached. First he became pastor of the New Bethel Baptist church on Willis and Hastings streets. A fairly big church, it was demolished to make way for a freeway. He went to another building—temporary quarters for his growing flock of followers, who loved his impassioned, musical style of preaching. Soon he moved to a church built for him. The "new" New Bethel Baptist church on Linwood Boulevard on Detroit's west side could hold 4,500 people.

Sometimes parishioners were overcome with emotion from his fiery messages, and nurses came to church on Sundays to help revive anyone who needed aid. Aretha and her brothers and sisters grew up in awe of their father. Not only did the sound of his preaching and talk-singing thrill Aretha, but she heard her mother's pretty voice singing the gospel hymns in church, too. Other gospel singers admired Barbara's voice. Rev. Franklin was invited by a friend to broadcast his sermons on a Detroit radio station. About eighty sermons were recorded. They were eventually licensed to Chess Records, a company that distributed them around the country. Then Baptists everywhere wanted to see and hear the preacher in person. Rev. Franklin began traveling to speak as a guest in other churches. He would eventually command four thousand dollars for a single appearance as a traveling evangelist.[2]

Rev. Franklin and his family seemed to have everything they could want. They were showered with respect. They were well known in the community. Parishioners filled his collection plate with money. The family lived in a big yellow brick house shaded by trees on LaSalle Boulevard. Rev. Franklin and his wife were blessed with five attractive, healthy children. The eldest, Barbara's son Vaughn by her first marriage, would become a career man in the U.S. Air

Force. Erma, the eldest daughter, had musical talent. Cecil liked the church and would become an assistant pastor. Aretha would show off her musical talent at an early age when she started playing the piano for the joy of it. Her baby sister, Carolyn, had musical talent, too. Along with Aretha, Erma and Carolyn would become professional singers, and Carolyn could also write songs.

But a shocking event rocked the family when Aretha was only six years old. Her mother left the family. Her departure would be forever shrouded in mystery. Neither Aretha nor anyone else in the family would say why Barbara Franklin disappeared. The only certain thing is that she left all her children with her husband. She died four years later in 1952. Aretha was ten years old. For his article about Aretha in *Vanity Fair*, James T. Jones IV talked with Willie Todd, a deacon of the New Bethel Baptist church, who said, "Reverend was gone so much. He was a playboy. I mean, truth is the light. That wasn't their first separation. . . ."[3] Musicians growing up in Detroit recall seeing Rev. Franklin in the Flame Show Bar, one of the many busy clubs in town at that time. They knew that some women found him attractive, and he enjoyed their attention. He loved the good things in life.

On the bright side, the gregarious minister attracted admirers among some of the most talented and fascinating African-Americans in the country. One was the legendary gospel singer Mahalia Jackson, who was often a guest in the big yellow brick house. She knew the Franklins so well that when she visited, she walked straight into the kitchen and started boiling a pot of collard greens for the family to eat. Rev. Franklin welcomed her assistance. He hired housekeepers to help him raise his brood, and the servants were especially necessary when he went on the road to preach the gospel. Mahalia Jackson noticed how saddened the children were after Barbara Franklin left them behind. Miss Jackson said, "The whole family wanted for love."[4]

Mahalia Jackson, who became known as the world's greatest gospel singer, frequently visited the Franklin house in Detroit when Aretha was a child.

More than ten years after Barbara Franklin's death, a pianist named Teddy Harris would play accompaniment for Aretha in her group. He and his family had always been friendly with the Franklins, and he thought that Aretha was always the sort of person who needed a lot of love. If she wasn't getting it from her first husband, she would seek it from the musicians in her group. "She just didn't like to be alone at all," he observed about the young woman. Although there were times when she seemed very happy, she was more often sad as a child and a young woman.

For publication, Aretha said almost nothing about her mother. "She was the choirmistress and pianist," Aretha told Jones for *Vanity Fair*. "I was so small when she was singing. I don't remember everything. But I knew she could sing and I certainly could see how much people enjoyed it."

Gospel singer Mavis Staples, whose friendship with the Franklins dated back to their earliest days in Detroit, recalled that Aretha "had a brush and a case. And I asked, 'That's your mother's brush?' And she said, 'Yeah, man, that's my mother's brush. It's still got a little hair in it.' I think that was the worst thing that could've happened for her, not to know her mother."[5] Aretha's grandmother had a hand in raising and disciplining the Franklin children. "She didn't spare the rod with any of us," Aretha has recalled. "You had to be doing it right with Big Mama or she would meet you at the nerve endings you would understand the most."[6]

Aretha went to the Alger Elementary School and finally to Northern High School. Soon after her mother left, Aretha's love for music blossomed. Mahalia Jackson would always tell people that Barbara Franklin had been a talented gospel singer with a beautiful voice. Though Aretha had a round face, and her mother's was long like her son Cecil's, Aretha seems to have inherited her mother's long nose, which was finely arched in profile, and slightly slanted, expressive eyes. (A photo of Barbara Franklin appeared on an American Masters documentary made for

Mavis Staples of the gospel group The Staple Singers
was a close friend of the Franklin family for decades.

television called "Aretha Franklin: the Queen of Soul," in 1988.) Both Aretha and her mother bore a vague resemblance to Nefertiti, an ancient Egyptian queen. Aretha would eventually keep a picture of Nefertiti on a wall of her house. She would dress in a Nefertiti costume for a party she gave there. Writer Mark Bego, who visited Aretha's house in suburban Bloomfield Hills, near Detroit, learned that the Egyptian queen was the Queen of Soul's favorite historical figure.

Rev. Franklin wielded positive, measureless authority over the children. In the African-American community, the Baptist minister was more important than the president of the United States. Not far away from their house was a neighborhood filled with people who lived on the edge of the law—the numbers men, pimps, hustlers, prostitutes, drug sellers, and drug users. These people held no allure and presented no role models for the young Franklin brood. They were attracted to the entertainers their father brought home. Sometimes, at midnight, he would wake up Aretha and coax the sleepy child downstairs to sing for the professional show people he had invited to the house after they finished working in clubs and theaters.

To Mark Bego, Aretha said, "We were very good kids. We. . .sat on the back porch. . .and told a lot of jokes late into the midnight hours. I had a piano right off the back porch, and sometimes I'd sing. . .all day, every day, with my sisters and my friends. Mostly what we heard on the radio—the Drifters, La Vern Baker, Ruth Brown. Oh, it was real nice. Of course in the end we'd argue, because we were tired. And I wanted to sing all through the night."[7]

Once she was playing the piano in earnest, using her own raw talent to instruct herself, she started learning from the celebrities who visited. In addition to Mahalia came gospel singers Clara Ward and the Reverend James Cleveland, the great blues singer B.B. King, jazz pianist Dorothy Donegan, and singers Dinah Washington and Arthur Prysock, Lou Rawls and Sam Cooke. Sometimes

Aretha sat quietly in a corner and listened to them. Rev. Cleveland taught her to explore music. "He showed me some real nice chords, and I liked his deep, deep sound. There's a whole lot of earthiness in the way he sings and what he was feeling," she would tell interviewers, as she began to develop a career.[8]

It was the pretty gospel singer Clara Ward who made the biggest impression on Aretha at first. Ward, well-known for her eye-catching costumes, sang the hymn "Peace in the Valley" with great fervor at a funeral for one of Aretha's aunts. Clara Ward was so carried away that she pulled her hat off and threw it on the ground. "From then on I knew what I wanted to do—sing!" Aretha said.[9]

After she sang her first solo in church, Aretha became a celebrity with her father's congregation. She kept playing piano, soloing, and singing in a gospel quartet with her sister Erma. Rev. Franklin gave Aretha many recordings to listen to, including Mahalia's and Clara Ward's. Mahalia's rich contralto and profound emotionalism made a deep impression on Aretha. But she copied every nuance of Miss Ward's piano playing and singing. "I thought one day she might decide she didn't want to play. . .and I'd be ready," Aretha described her early ambition.

Aretha also loved to go roller skating to the sound of popular music at the nearby Arcadia Roller Rink. Her father sweetly rewarded her service as a soloist in church by paying her fifteen dollars a week—a good, usual sum in those days. She saved her money. "I bought my first pair of roller skates with Raybestos wheels. They were about thirty dollars a wheel, so I had to really save for those skates," she told writer Mark Bego. She also liked to spend time with her father, eating ice cream and watching boxing matches on television. She was especially enthralled by the handsome, classy, middleweight boxing champion, Sugar Ray Robinson.

But even as an adolescent, she had a sense of apartness. In school, her marks were As, Bs, and Cs. There was

*Clara Ward, a premier gospel singer, fascinated Aretha.
After hearing Clara sing and seeing her throw her hat
on the ground at a funeral, Aretha knew she wanted
to be a singer, too.*

an occasional D—but never in music. She was often called out of her classes because the auditorium teacher needed someone to help control a class that had gotten too wild and high-spirited, throwing spitballs or fighting. "I'd have to play the piano to entertain. . .I hated that," Aretha recalled for Mark Bego. "I really wanted to get down with the kids and do a little screaming myself, but I had to sing. That was my first experience with a tough audience."

During the summers, Aretha joined her father's evangelist road shows. He traveled by plane, and his children and the rest of his entourage covered long distances by bus, going to the South and California. "Driving eight or ten hours, trying to make a gig, and being hungry and passing restaurants all along the road, and having to go off the highway into some little city to find a place to eat because you're black—that had its effect," Aretha's brother Cecil would recall of the exhausting trips.

A bright note was that the kids could always rely upon their father to pay them for their work. Promoters of gospel shows couldn't always be counted on to pay the travelers on the gospel highway, but their father could be. Also, Rev. Franklin's fans around the country offered his group places where they could eat and sleep. That refuge helped the Franklin children relax. And if they stayed in hotels and motels where they knew they would be welcome, they often met rhythm and blues stars and other entertainers. When the entertainers passed through Detroit, they went to the magnetic minister's yellow brick house for hospitality and collard greens.

"I traveled from about the age of thirteen to sixteen with my dad," Aretha would recall, "singing with the Roberta Martin singers, the Clara Ward Singers Caravan—real gospel giants. It was great training." In that period, she also became friends with the gospel world's Staple Singers, another well-known group, including Mavis Staples.

Aretha's father encouraged her to overcome her stage fright. "Take your time; say what you want to say," he told her, as Mark Bego recounted in his biography of Aretha.[10] Though all the Franklin girls had musical talent, Rev. Franklin gave practical encouragement and unflagging support to Aretha in particular. In the American Masters documentary on her life broadcast on PBS, Aretha would sum up: "I think my dad thought I was gifted and uniquely talented as a child."[11] When Aretha was fourteen, at a church service in Oakland, California, she recorded two gospel songs, "Never Grow Old" and "Precious Lord, Take My Hand," for Chess Records, a company known for its gospel recordings. Aretha tried to copy every detail and innuendo of Clara Ward's gospel singing style.

Then Aretha went back to the New Bethel Baptist Church in Detroit, where Chess recorded more of her performances and released them as an album, *Songs of Faith*. She inspired the congregation to shout for her: "Amen!", "Oh Lord!", and "Listen at her!" Years later, a record producer for Atlantic, Jerry Wexler, would be so charmed by the man who yelled "Listen at her!" that Wexler would use the phrase as the title of a chapter about Aretha in his autobiography.

On the road with her father, singing one or two songs before his sermons, Aretha earned fifty dollars for each performance. "It was exciting," she would recall. Her contacts with pop and blues artists on the road and in her Detroit neighborhood also stimulated her. She bought recordings by Fats Domino and Bobby Blue Bland; the King of Soul, Ray Charles; and Ruth Brown.

Within blocks of her house lived many talented young musicians. They would grow up to be famous pop stars and accomplished jazz musicians. Among them were Otis Williams of the group the Temptations, and the international stars Diana Ross, Florence Ballard, and Mary Wilson, who formed the Supremes. Mary Wilson thought

Aretha had the gift of making people feel they were listening to superb music, not just gospel music. That was why her gospel-based music pleased everybody. Stardom-bound Smokey Robinson, whose family was friendly with the Franklins, was amazed at how Aretha achieved her driving, two-fisted piano style at an early age. She learned to accompany herself dramatically with delicate, subtle runs and sophisticated chords, all rooted in an insistently rhythmic gospel style.

Aretha admired the rhythm and blues singers as much as they admired her gospel singing. For her, the most exciting pop singer to visit her house was Dinah Washington. Dinah went there at different times with a Detroit man-about-town, Ted White. In his mid-twenties when Aretha was in her mid-teens, White was a "player"—a man with many enterprises and ways to earn money. "He was a handsome, charming, intelligent man," said one musician who knew Ted White well, with all his strengths and short-comings, in those days. "He could charm any woman. He had the gift of gab." Though Ted would have a major influence on Aretha later on, at their first meeting they barely noticed each other. Dinah was Aretha's idol. She loved Dinah's style, sound, musicality, and versatility.

Also very important to Aretha when she was a teenager was the gospel singer Sam Cooke, who traveled from Chicago to sing at Rev. Franklin's church. Aretha developed a crush on him. Mark Bego would report that she said, "Oh, I loved that man. I was a great Sam Cooke fan. I had a little book on everything on him, down to his Kent cigarettes." (She saved an empty pack he left behind.) "He was young, handsome and quite dashing. He was a very down-to-earth and beautiful person."[12]

Switching from a gospel to a pop singing career, Sam sang at the Flame Show Bar. Aretha was too young to be admitted there when Sam made a record, "You Send Me." So he brought it to the house for her to hear. Aretha loved all the nuances of his voice and his control of

Dinah Washington: As a teenager, Aretha met Dinah Washington, the inspiring pop, blues, and jazz singer, who called herself the "Queen of the Blues."

dynamics. When Sam's song became a pop and rhythm and blues hit, Aretha felt convinced that she would like to become a pop singer.

A few men in town were launching a new recording company called Motown. It had a characteristic sound—a combination of rhythm and blues, rock and roll, and pop music—that would refresh popular music and bring talented African-Americans into the mainstream. The Supremes were one of Motown's very successful groups. Aretha, at age fifteen, wanted to record for the new company. But her father disliked the idea of her getting into the music business when she was so young. He let her play as a pianist to accompany her elder sister Erma, who started rehearsing in a Motown studio. Erma wanted to be a jazz singer, however, and so she never actually made a recording for Motown. Neither did Aretha. "All the children were very much under the influence of their father," recalls Teddy Harris, the Detroit pianist who would work as one of Aretha's long-term accompanists. The Franklin children didn't generally defy Rev. C. L. Franklin.

Aretha did, however, do something that year that neither she nor any one in the family had expected. She became pregnant. And the identity of the father of Aretha's first son remained a mystery and a secret as well guarded by the family as the reason for Barbara Franklin's disappearance. Aretha named him Clarence, in honor of her father.

As far as anyone knows, Aretha didn't love anyone more than she did her idol Sam Cooke. It's not completely unreasonable to speculate that she and Sam Cooke had a love affair. Some people thought that. Aretha knew about the speculation and denied it was true. Whoever the father was, Aretha didn't marry him. She left school and withdrew into the family circle in the big yellow brick house. It was not a revolutionary thing for a teenage girl to have a child at that time. Many of Aretha's friends did it. Birth control pills weren't available in those days. Her

Sam Cooke sang in a gospel quartet, then switched to popular music. When Aretha was still too young to go to clubs, he brought her his hit record "You Send Me." She had a crush on the handsome young man, and his success as a pop and rhythm and blues singer persuaded her to sing secular music.

father, a prominent churchman, could have become extremely angry or embarrassed. Instead, he sheltered her. To heighten the mystery, increase her aura of rebelliousness, and perhaps test her father's mettle even more, Aretha, at seventeen, had another son, whom she named Edward. Again, the father's identity was never made public.

As an unwed teenage mother, Aretha might have had to abandon her dreams of becoming a singer to raise her children, if she hadn't been the beloved daughter of an influential, worldly-wise Baptist minister. Prominent in the National Baptist Association, with several million members, he was not the sort of man to close his door on his own children while he kept it open to so many other people.

In return, Aretha respected her father completely. "Her father was the boss. The children deferred to him— very much so," recalls Jerry Wexler.[13] He was the record company executive and producer at Atlantic who would have the greatest impact on Aretha's career in the years ahead. The children became actually "psychologically dependent" upon the forceful Rev. Franklin, Wexler said, adding: "The great, spellbinding preacher had his children spellbound. Aretha gave him great deference. She honored her father."[14]

So, although she had burdened herself with two babies, she had listened well to her father's message that success or failure in life depended upon a person's mental attitude. She really wanted to succeed, make him proud of her, and be proud of herself. A soft-voiced youngster, who presented a shy, polite personality to the public, she soon decided to take charge of her life—with a little more help from her father.

THREE

ARETHA GOES
TO NEW YORK

❝ ▌ let [my father] know I wanted to change from gospel
to pop. He told me that if this was what I wanted to
do, then this is what I should do," Aretha would say for
the PBS documentary.[1] Her father's congregation was
upset, taking the traditional view that she was either turning
her back on the church or else on God.

"My father played quite an influential role in elevat-
ing the people's enlightenment," said her brother Cecil
about their father's steadfastness on Aretha's behalf.[2] Rev.
Franklin helped her make practical plans for a career. They
talked about which record label they should approach.
His gospel world connections would help him pave the
way out of the yellow brick house for Aretha, who was
eighteen in 1960.

By then, Sam Cooke was an important recording star
for RCA. The legend was that he wanted her to sign with
his company. He was so influential that, if she had agreed
to sign with RCA, he could have just nodded his head at
the executives and they would have signed her. But
Columbia, another major label, appealed to the Franklins.

"So we went to New York. I lived in the Big Apple,"
Aretha would sum up the most crucial journey of her life so

far.[3] In New York, she began to meet people who respected her talent and helped open doors. A jazz bassist named Major Holley, a family friend from Detroit, took her to clubs to hear music and introduced her to people he knew. Major, too, came from a musically gifted family. It was a special pleasure for him to try to help the nice, wholesome-looking young woman.

People who knew Aretha at that time recall she was sometimes chaperoned by an older woman—probably an artist's manager named Jo Basil King. She took on Aretha as a client. And Aretha went into a recording studio and played piano and sang in her sweet, emotion-packed, clear soprano with her excellent enunciation. She chose the song "Today I Sing the Blues," and infused it with an underpinning of gospel feeling. The recording made it clear that she could do anything with her voice. Jo King passed the demonstration tape to John Hammond, a very important and unusual record producer at Columbia.

He was related to a very wealthy American family, the Vanderbilts, who had made a fortune in railroading. He had a small trust fund, and for a large part of his life he would rely upon that for some of his income. He probably could have used his family's connections to find a job in society circles. But he had fallen in love with music from the African-American culture—blues first, then jazz—and he devoted his life to music and musicians. Without taking a percentage of their profits, he kept bringing great blues and jazz artists into Columbia's studios and making recordings that would become classics. His first love among the blues singers was Bessie Smith, who was called "Empress of the Blues."

In 1933, when Bessie was making her last recordings, John Hammond had gone to a club in Harlem and discovered another singer—the enigmatic and soft-voiced Billie Holiday with her laid-back, lazy sense of rhythm and bluesy melodic style. He thought she was the greatest singer he had heard since Bessie. So he brought Billie into

Record producer and talent scout John Hammond thought Aretha had the greatest voice he had heard since he had discovered Billie Holiday. He arranged for Aretha to sign a contract with Columbia.

a studio to record for the first time with clarinetist Benny Goodman. He would become known as the "King of Swing" and present the first jazz concert at Carnegie Hall. When Jo King arranged for Hammond to hear Aretha's demonstration tape, she gave him a new lease on life. "My God, that's the greatest voice I've heard since Billie Holiday," he said. Hearing the rumor that Hammond loved Aretha's voice, Jo King invited him to her studio to meet Aretha. He signed her to a six-year recording contract with Columbia. "I made some good records with Aretha," he would reminisce as part of the American Masters documentary. "I wanted to keep her to a degree as a jazz singer. But Columbia wanted to make her a pop singer. I thought that would ruin her integrity."[4]

Thus began six years of confusion at Columbia. The company's executives heard how beautiful and affecting her voice was, and she could do everything so well that nobody could decide what style she should concentrate on. They asked her to sing everything, from pop songs to standards by the great composers for Broadway musical theater, to the blues, rock and roll, rhythm and blues, and jazz classics.

At that time, John Hammond was working with one of his young discoveries, jazz pianist Ray Bryant, from a music- and church-oriented family in Philadelphia; his mother was a Pentecostal minister. Ray had recently become a star with a hit instrumental record called "Little Susie." Hammond staged a party for Aretha at a club called the Village Vanguard, a long-established, important club featuring jazz in New York. Once the party was in full swing, Hammond telephoned Ray to come to the club and meet Aretha. Her father chaperoned her that night. Ray and Aretha performed together and immediately established artistic communication. "That girl can sing," Ray thought. Offstage, in her sweet-voiced, naive way, Aretha let Ray know how much she wanted to succeed in the music business. He owned a new Cadillac, which she admired. She told him that she hoped to be able to buy one for herself. He assured her that there was no reason why she should not be a success.

That August 1960, Hammond arranged for Aretha to record with Ray's group for her first album. Aretha knew how good the musicians were—all professional jazzmen. One was bassist Bill Lee, whose son Spike, would become one of the first nationally famous African-American filmmakers. Quentin Jackson, a trombonist with Duke Ellington's orchestra, played for Aretha in the group, too.

John Hammond invited Art D'Lugoff, who owned the popular jazz club the, Village Gate, to come to Columbia's offices and listen to her first album, called *Aretha*. D'Lugoff was so impressed that he booked her immediately. She alternated sets with Horace Silver, a soulful pianist and composer, who was leading his own featured group. One of Silver's musicians, a Detroit-born drummer named Roy Brooks, thought she sounded strong, clear, and powerful the first time he heard her, and she would always sound that way to him. Once he got to know her, he liked and admired her personally. "Her father set [that Columbia recording connection] up for her, and she went on from there. And she was always good to musicians from Detroit, hiring them for her groups," he said.[5] At the Village Gate, D'Lugoff asked Aretha to come back for more appearances. The audiences loved her. Nina Simone, then a very popular young singer, came to hear Aretha. D'Lugoff thought that Nina was very impressed by how well Aretha sang. D'Lugoff thought Nina may have even been startled by the competition Aretha suddenly presented.

Aretha never set up a third date for herself at the Gate. She was shy, musicians thought at that time. And Ted Fox, author of a book called *Showtime at the Apollo*, the history of that legendary black theater in Harlem, confirmed it. He wrote: "[She] was insecure about her abilities and not comfortable with the pop market strategy

Trombonist Tyree Glenn played with Aretha in a group led by pianist Ray Bryant (not shown here) at Aretha's first recording session for Columbia in August 1960. Curtis Lewis is the man in the middle.

Columbia's top artists-and-repertoire man, Mitch Miller, had mapped out for her. She ran away from recording sessions. 'When I first recorded *Aretha* in 1960,' said John Hammond, 'I twisted [the arm of the owner of the Apollo] and he hired her because she had a couple of successful records. She didn't show up until the third day. He held me personally responsible.' "6

The Schiffman family, which owned the Apollo, applauded her talent, however. So did the Apollo audience, which loved her singing "Evil Gal Blues"—a song that her idol, Dinah Washington, had become famous for. Aretha's delivery was vital, with her soulful, powerful voice high-flying and squalling. She sounded as if she was born to sing the material—the gospel-rooted treatment of the melody, the blues form with its repeated lines, and "the devil's words."

I'm an evil gal. . .
If you tell me good morning,
I'm gonna tell you that's a lie. . .
If you want to be happy,
Don't you mess around with me
If you want to be happy,
Don't you mess around with me,
Because I'll empty your pockets
And fill you with misery. . .7

In Fox's book, there's a charming photograph of a young, slender Aretha dressed in a dancer's leotard, taking a lesson from a well-known tap dancer, Cholly Atkins. Such lessons helped her build confidence and acquire stagecraft; she needed to move with poise on stage.

Aretha traveled back and forth between Detroit and New York for a while; first she lived in the YWCA on East 38th Street, then moved into Jo King's midtown apartment. In addition to dance lessons with Atkins, Aretha studied voice with vocal coach Leora Carter. Sometimes at night

To learn poise and stagecraft, Aretha studied dance with choreographer Cholly Atkins around the time she first appeared at the Apollo Theater in the early 1960s.

Aretha went out to hear music with Major Holley. "That was great," she would recall about time spent with the amusing and protective musician who helped ease her into the New York scene.

A music reviewer, possibly for the *Village Voice*, was pleasantly surprised by Aretha's first recording for Columbia. He ranked her with Nancy Wilson and Gloria Lynne, two very popular singers, who also had new recordings out at that time. The reviewer called Aretha unsophisticated but impassioned. He knew about John Hammond's "ardor" for his new discovery. "I've been waiting for a girl like this for twenty years," Hammond told the reviewer.[8] The reviewer didn't want to be influenced by the important producer's praise. But as soon as he heard the record, he wrote, "We are happy to report. . .that our reservations were quickly swept away by the sheer uncomplicated fervor of this girl. She sings gospel/blues material, of which this album is essentially comprised, in a delightful, open, uninhibited, totally involved manner, communicating strongly, realizing the potential of this type of music. Backgrounds by pianist Ray Bryant's trio, with added soloists Quentin 'Butter' Jackson, trombone, Al Sears, tenor sax, and 'Lord' Westbrook, guitar, substantially aid Miss Franklin's cause." [9]

Another reviewer, Barbara Gardner, in *Down Beat* magazine, gave Aretha's first album four stars—the highest possible rating, saying, "Aretha Franklin is the most important female vocalist to come along in some years." Gardner added that Aretha was a challenge to Dinah Washington, the Queen of the Blues. "Miss Franklin has the pipes and the soul." Gardner heard the church-rooted, gospel-tinged legacy of Ray Charles, too, in Aretha's singing.

Her audition song, "Today I Sing the Blues," included in her first album, climbed in the pop charts to become one of the Top Ten rhythm and blues recordings. "Won't Be Long," a gospel-based tune on the album, also ranked among the Top Ten rhythm and blues (r&b) songs, and it crossed over to become number 76 in the pop charts. The r&b chart measured the popularity of songs that had once been called race music—records done by and for African-Americans. The pop charts reflected the choices of whites. Although white and African-American musicians were the first groups in America to integrate and respect each other's talents, segregation had permeated the business end of the music industry. African-Americans, who invented gospel, the blues, and jazz, needed hits on the pop charts to reach the widest possible market, fulfill their sales potential, and become successful and wealthy. Though the odds were against them, many African-American musicians managed to become stars and raise the consciousness of the nation. "The green dollar and the black song did more to eliminate segregation than all the polemics and preaching in the world," as Jerry Wexler would view the influence of African-American musicians.[10]

With his astute taste and sensibility, pianist Ray Bryant recognized right away that Aretha had her own style. He thought that nobody else's voice sounded quite like hers. Columbia could present her in any musical setting, with any type of musical accompaniment, but she would still sound individualistic. Ray played with her at a little club called The Jazz Gallery on St. Mark's Place in Greenwich Village. But he was a jazz-oriented group leader. Aretha was trying to find her own signature style and stand on her own. Ray went off in his own direction. She started performing and recording with many other musicians, sometimes playing piano for herself.

She understood harmonies, melodies, and rhythms; she knew exactly what to play for her expressive voice. She began to have turntable hits—songs that the disk jockeys played a lot on the air, but none had great sales. Even so, there were no better interpretations of some of the songs than Aretha's versions. Her voice was high and clear, rich and nubile. At times she sounded like a pop singer, but all the while, for anyone who listened closely, her gospel roots, and the creative imagination for improvisation that could distinguish a gospel singer as a unique stylist, constituted her greatest strengths. Dizzy Gillespie, the brilliant trumpeter who, with Charlie "Bird" Parker, invented the jazz style called "bebop," said, "Nobody could write down all the notes that Aretha sings."

John Hammond aimed her work at a jazz audience, and jazz fans rewarded her by appreciating her work. *Down Beat* magazine named her its new female vocal star of the year in the 1961 International Jazz Critics Poll. That year, she made her second album, *The Electrifying Aretha Franklin*, on which she sang a tune once made famous by old-time jazz vaudeville star Al Jolson—"Rock-a-bye Your Baby with a Dixie Melody." With it, Aretha landed on the Top 40 pop singles chart.

She also toured the country with her own group. Still young and uncertain of herself, she found some clubs too funky—rundown and actually frightening. They were a far cry from the sheltering New Bethel Baptist Church, where she had waited her turn in a high-backed, regal-looking chair. In clubs, Aretha was "afraid," she said, and sometimes sang "to the floor."[11]

On one of her trips back to Detroit, she again met the charming, handsome, older man, Ted White, in a nightclub. They had overlooked each other when he visited her father's house with Dinah Washington. But now Aretha was a grown woman with a recording contract. White's friends knew that many women found him irresistible. He was enterprising and intelligent, and he had a sense of humor. But he had a reputation for wildness, which made him seem like the exact opposite of Aretha's church-centered father. Yet Aretha fell in love with Ted. Friends of both White and the Franklins are sure that Rev. Franklin opposed the marriage. Nevertheless Aretha made up her mind that Ted White was the man for her. Once again her father did not withdraw his love and support from his daughter. Ted White was eleven years older than she, and he had the self-confidence to give her a boost when she did the difficult work of traveling to work in clubs, many of them in the inner cities, around the country.

Aretha's family raised her two sons in Detroit, while she, Ted, and the musicians he had hired for her group went on the road. They were not the musicians with whom she recorded in the studios. Ted became her manager, guiding many of her decisions. When Aretha became pregnant, she worked up until the last months. They named their son, Teddy, Jr. Because the tours made Aretha so tired, after a while Ted tried to arrange for her to go on the road for two weeks, then rest for two weeks with him and Teddy, Jr., at their house on Sorrento Street in Detroit.

But life for the Whites wasn't restful anyplace. Aretha had two struggles going on. She was trying—and failing—to make records that sold a million copies and qualified as platinum, or at least gold records that sold half a million copies. Only her rankings in the polls were good, sometimes very good, sometimes not. At the same time, as a young, inexperienced wife, Aretha was trying to cope with her husband's forceful character. At Columbia, several producers felt that Ted was interfering with her career by telling her what to do. John Hammond simply said that Aretha had terrible luck with men. Another producer suggested that Ted meant well, but neither he nor anyone else came up with any solutions about her commercial appeal. The problem was probably not Ted at all but the general confusion about Aretha's career at Columbia. But she and Ted fought often about many things.

"Everybody knew it was a difficult marriage," said one family friend. Another, who played in Aretha's group and liked both Ted White and Rev. Franklin, went to a party at her house. Rev. Franklin and Ted White began to argue. "They never got along," the musician said. The fight became so heated that the men threatened each other's safety. "That let me know they didn't respect each other," the musician said.

Aretha, in her twenties in this picture, was already being guided by her longtime, loyal friend, Ruth Bowen, of the Queens Booking Corporation in New York.

Another musician, Teddy Harris, who was aware of how much Aretha and Ted fought, thought their arguments were almost silly. They could be about anything. Still another musician, who would play in Aretha's group when she left Columbia and went to record for Atlantic, thought that Ted White was a man who would not have been good at loving any woman in those days. Later in life, Ted would seem to be a changed man, a businessman in the Detroit area, living a quiet life. But when he and Aretha were married, they created fireworks. Teddy Harris told writer Jones for *Vanity Fair* that Ted White "was kind of abusive" to Aretha.[12]

She and Ted did have at least one thing in common: they had the same birthday, March 25, eleven years apart. "Two Aries," said several musicians, explaining that the couple's conflicts were written in their stars. (Musicians, whose artistry stems from the wordless spirit, almost always believe in a higher force—God—which allows the music to pass through them, and they are fascinated with all sorts of mystical and spiritual ideas, including astrology.)

Aretha had cause to be upset by other events in those years. Teddy Harris would never forget the night in 1964 that the group was performing at Pasquale's Carousel in Atlanta, Georgia, when they got the news that Aretha's friend Sam Cooke had been murdered in a motel. He had been behaving very strangely. The motel owner had shot him. "Aretha went berserk," Teddy Harris recalled. "After all the customers and employees had gone home from the club, she made all of the musicians in her group stay with her there, and she played Sam Cooke's music on the piano for four hours. And she drank, too, with us."

And while her recording career was having its ups and downs, it's not clear how much authority she had in choosing the songs she recorded. She always liked to sing songs that she could relate to events in her own life. She recorded one song about keeping her spirits up during the day and then crying all night into her pillow—a song she understood very well, because she and Ted fought so much. Though she was singing varied material, so much of it was jazz-oriented that Aretha was regarded as a bright young traditional jazz singer. She starred at the Newport Jazz Festival in Rhode Island and the New York Jazz Festival on Randall's Island in New York. On the bills with her were Duke Ellington at Newport and Dizzy Gillespie at Randall's Island, among other jazz stars. But the prestigious bookings were not the same thing as great record sales. Aretha never really wanted to be a jazz singer.

When John Hammond went away on a vacation, another producer, Al Kasha, made a single record with Aretha called "Operation Heartbreak." It went into the Top Ten on the r&b singles list. After that, Hammond was never given a chance to produce albums with her. Columbia's executives may have been searching for a producer who could help her with record sales. Producers themselves may have wanted to try their luck with a potential star—an attractive, fresh-faced youngster with a remarkable voice. Even though she doubted herself, she had a confident stage presence from her years as a star at her father's church.

She made ten albums for the company between 1960 and 1966. Important people in the recording industry, critics, audiences, and disk jockeys had their favorite songs by Aretha. Some people loved an album called *Unforgettable*, which she made in tribute to the "Queen of the Blues," Dinah Washington, released in 1964, not long after Dinah died.

For an album produced by Robert Mersey, Aretha sang a tune called "Soulville." It had an element missing from many of her Columbia recordings. Perhaps if that element—a percussive, rhythmically regular, musical background—had been employed more, she would have gone further toward becoming a superstar at Columbia. But as Jerry Wexler, the man who would soon become pivotal for Aretha's career at Atlantic, says, "perhaps" doesn't mean anything, when all the votes are in.[15]

Recordings that Aretha made with producer Clyde Otis were very fine. They included such titles as "Love For Sale," in a decidedly jazzy, uptempo interpretation—one of the best recordings ever made of that song, and one of her best recordings ever. It proved that she was one of the greatest jazz singers, just as she was a great gospel, blues, and pop singer. "Muddy Water" was another song that Aretha delivered with the perfect tempo and feeling. Clyde Otis had her on a good track, for at least she was singing with the spirit that she had brought with her from the New Bethel Baptist Church. Another song, "Runnin' Out of Fools," featured Aretha telling a contemporary story in a charged, soulful way about a man calling her after such a long time that she bet he couldn't even remember what she looked like. She thought he must be looking through his little black book and digging deep into his past, because he was running out of fools to call and try to impress. She sounded so soulful, as she also did on a song which she had written with Ted White, "Take It Like You Give It."

Aretha's career at Columbia established her as a major talent, but she was left waiting in the wings for stardom, and she was very unhappy about being overlooked. Ed Sullivan, host of the most popular television show at the time, booked her as a guest. She showed up in a low-cut gown that had been custom-made for her appearance. The show's censors said it was too revealing. She switched to a gown with a high neck. But Sullivan's staff had overbooked the show. By the time she dressed a second time, it was over. She never got onstage and left the studio in tears.

When Columbia executives couldn't find the magic formula to launch her into her proper orbit, they let her career coast along. They had modeled her after people who had come before her. There's also a legend that Ted White interfered with Clyde Otis's ideas for promoting Aretha. Her album *Runnin' Out of Fools*, produced by

Otis, became her second highest charting album, including her second highest charting single. Otis wanted to keep her singing the same soulful songs. But, he said, Ted White wanted to promote her as a versatile artist and a jazz singer. The men clashed. As Otis would recall for the PBS documentary, in the American Masters series, he told White: "Why don't you just let her do what she wants to do?"[16]

Aretha didn't know what that was yet. She told an interviewer that she was still trying to find out who she was. Certainly, throughout her years at Columbia, she hadn't decided yet to insist on a bombastic style that struck sparks and sent out songs as veritable little commandos for change in the pop music world. Columbia actually tried to downplay her gospel roots. It was a white-oriented company for white-style music, many people inside and outside the company would later say.

Furthermore, the early 1960s was the wrong time to promote Aretha as an old-fashioned jazz singer—the interpreter of a softer, older music that Columbia had become famous for. All the great jazz singers had established themselves by the 1950s. After that tastes in popular music began moving away from jazz. Jazz was becoming a complex art music. The Beatles and other pop groups were dominating the music charts, performing simpler music. They were writing their own songs, and they announced that they took their inspiration from the southern blues singers and musicians. They were Aretha's spiritual musical kin, too. And they appealed to pop music fans, who wanted to clap, and stomp, and let their hair down—"let it all hang out."

The civil rights movement and other revolutionary changes were putting pressure on society. The elemental music that was deep in Aretha's spirit mirrored the mood of the people. She shared the emotions of her own people, who were fighting with practical and intellectual

The inspiration for the civil rights movement, Rev. Martin Luther King, Jr., was leading a march from Selma to Montgomery, Alabama, in March 1965. On his left is his wife, Coretta Scott King. On his right is Dr. Ralph Bunche, and the first man to Dr. Bunche's right is Rev. Ralph Abernathy.

methods in the courts, and sometimes with violent confrontations in public places, to integrate buses, lunch counters, the workforce—the world. Some African-Americans were dying for equal rights; some worked in revolutionary groups. So did some white people. Everyone wanted a change, either for the goals of racial equality, or for social justice for all, or to end the war in Vietnam, or for individual liberties, or even for radical change for its own sake. A women's movement was beginning to emerge. All around Aretha, times were changing. And Columbia didn't have the orientation of a rhythm and blues company to present her properly.

Though Columbia took the emphasis off her gospel roots, Aretha, on her own, did not. Totally apart from her recording career, she had sung at a concert held at Chicago's McCormack Place in 1963 "to honor the heroes of Birmingham, where scores of protesting schoolchildren had been attacked by police with dogs and fire hoses," James T. Jones IV recounted in his *Vanity Fair* article, quoting Taylor Branch's study of the civil rights movement, *Parting the Waters*. Rev. Martin Luther King spoke there. Then Mahalia Jackson, Dinah Washington, and Aretha sang. "The three of them," wrote Branch, "held the overflow crowd until two o'clock in the morning, when young Aretha Franklin topped them all with her closing hymn. Only twenty one. . .still four years away from crossover stardom as Lady Soul. . .she gave the whites in her audience a glimpse of the future. She wrung them all inside out with the Thomas Dorsey classic, 'Precious Lord, Take My Hand,' and by the time she finished few doubted that for one night they had held the most favored spot on earth."[17]

Aretha's embattled marriage with Ted White did nothing to help her decide for herself exactly what songs and style of music she should focus on for a pop career. It's not surprising that Ted White couldn't steer her career in the right direction. He was not a musical genius. Columbia's experienced producers couldn't make the miracle happen for her. And the company didn't promote her records enough. She was adrift, without expert management.

Aretha's time at Columbia wasn't wasted, however. She recorded beautiful songs, developed stamina, and acquired experience.

FOUR

ARETHA GOES TO ATLANTIC, THE RIGHT PLACE AT THE RIGHT TIME

A retha was willing to keep working to become a star. People might think she depended on the judgment of others, but it had been her decision to try to become a commercial success as a pop singer in the first place. She hadn't changed her mind.

Jerry Wexler, an executive at Atlantic Records, a small firm that specialized in rhythm and blues—the blues-based popular music of African-Americans—had heard Aretha's early gospel recordings for Chess Records. Throughout the 1960s, Wexler thought almost everything she did for Columbia was beautiful, even though it was plain to him that her career had no focus.

His company had been founded by Ahmet Ertegun, an emigrant from Turkey to America, and New Yorker Herb Abramson, who adored southern-style, African-American inspired music. Then Jerry Wexler became a partner, followed by Ahmet's brother, Nesuhi. Originally a jazz fan, Jerry Wexler had great talent as a scout for rhythm and blues artists and went right into the studios and worked with them. Sometimes he helped them write and arrange their music. He gave them ideas to encourage them to do whatever they wanted to do most of all, and to do it the

Jerry Wexler, a partner in Atlantic Records and a legendary talent scout and record producer for soul music, signed Aretha to his label, sat her down at the piano to perform her gospel-rooted soul music, and invited audiences to come to her. They came running.

best way they knew how. He supported the stars he chose to sign, for the poignant yet aggressive soul sound of the 1960s. According to Arif Mardin, a co-producer at Atlantic, Wexler provided his artists with some "tightly played horns and a great rhythm section playing danceable and hard rhythmic patterns."[1] They were steady, insistent, often simple rhythms, unlike the complex polyrhythms of jazz. Wexler's stars operated in the realm of the earthy and the nitty gritty, with amplification. With his enthusiasm and drive, he gave focus to his artists' careers and enjoyed the fruits of their commercial hits.

By 1966 he had gotten into the habit of leaving New York and going south to work in a recording studio called Fame. It was located in Muscle Shoals, Alabama, a small town near the Tennessee border. He loved the flavor of the music played by southern musicians. The whole scene refreshed him. In Muscle Shoals, he had found a group of white Southerners who had started out as country musicians. Then they had taken what he called "a left turn toward the blues."[2] So he brought his stars to Fame.

Normally life went smoothly there. However, one day, Wilson Pickett and Percy Sledge, Atlantic recording stars, got into a fight in the studio. When Wexler tried to break it up, Pickett threw him against a wall. At that moment, the phone rang. A woman named Louise Bishop, a disk jockey specializing in gospel music, was calling Wexler from Philadelphia. Louise was a friend of Aretha Franklin. Despite the variety of music Aretha had been singing, Jerry still thought of her as someone who "ran with the gospel crowd." Her father remained a bulwark of support for her. (He told her she would sing for "Kings and Queens" one day, she would confide in an audience much later.[3]) Wexler knew her contract with Columbia had ended. He wanted to sign Aretha to Atlantic. He had already signed such stars as Wilson Pickett and a soul group called Sam and Dave. Ray Charles and Ruth Brown

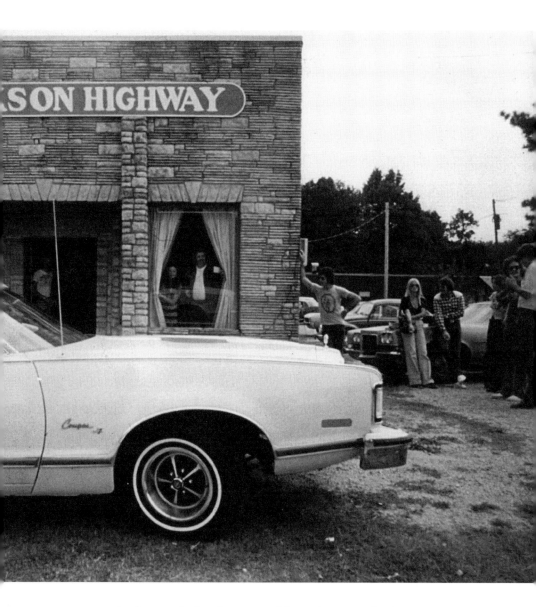

*Aretha made her first record for Atlantic at the Fame
studio in Muscle Shoals, Alabama.*

had recorded for Atlantic, too. Louise Bishop told Jerry that Aretha wanted to talk to him. He called her right away, and they set a meeting date. Her husband would come with her to Jerry's office in New York.

Aretha and Ted White showed up without a lawyer or anyone else in tow to complicate their thoughts and decisions. Aretha loved Jerry's enthusiasm for her singing. He knew she was going to do well, he told her. He was going to let her sing and shout and whisper the blues guided by the spirit of her gospel roots and her contemporary feeling for a song. He understood her gift. And she knew exactly the sort of company that Atlantic was. As a teenager buying records in Detroit, she had loved many of Atlantic's recording artists. Aretha felt special kinship with singers such as Brother Ray Charles. She was home free listening to Ruth Brown.

She and Ted White agreed to sign a contract with Atlantic for twenty-five thousand dollars—not a great deal of money. She had not proven herself to be a big money-maker yet, and she actually owed Columbia money from that company's investment in her. Wexler needed no encouragement to back up his own conviction about Aretha's commercial potential. His friend John Hammond congratulated him on signing Aretha: "You'll do good things with Aretha. You understand her musically." Hammond also told Wexler that Aretha was "enigmatic and withdrawn."

Wexler tried to get a producer in Memphis to work with Aretha for the Stax label, which was affiliated with Atlantic. But the people at Stax didn't want to pay the twenty-five thousand dollar advance. Wexler thought Stax could do a better job with Aretha than he could, and he was also extremely busy with his work and personal plans; he always had many projects going at once. For lack of an alternative, he decided to produce her records himself. Later he would be so happy that the Memphis producer had turned down the chance to work with Aretha. In his book, Wexler wrote about the way things turned out: "Thank you, Jesus."[4]

Aretha was then a grown woman—twenty-five years old and the mother of three sons. As all the blues singers did, she sang from her own experience, and that experience had been tough, complicated, and often unhappy. Wexler didn't know all the specific events of Aretha's earlier life. But he had a good idea about some of it. She had been exposed to the world very early, because her father was a famous preacher and a sophisticated man. Musicians often saw him at such places as the Flame Show Bar in Detroit. "That was a very unusual place for a minister to go," thought several musicians, including Hugh Lawson, a Detroit-born jazz pianist who played pool for recreation with Aretha's brother Cecil. Rev. Franklin also liked to go to nightclubs in other cities when he was on the road and finished with his church work for the day. A Detroit-born bassist, Herman Wright, saw Rev. Franklin come into the Southerland Lounge on the south side of Chicago several times. "He liked music. He frequented clubs. He had an active life," Wright said. "Reverend Franklin was a real nice man, a smooth guy, a masterful speaker, and he was always well dressed in a tasteful suit and tie."[5] Rev. Franklin had complimented Wright on his playing.

The minister never sheltered his children from people, events, and ideas. Wexler knew that Aretha had never been kept in an ivory tower. As the child of a Baptist minister, she had grown up in the center of a community that was, in many ways, a little country, where her father was chief of state. She knew precisely what was going on in the lives of the people in the "country." A church in the inner city is not a spiritual retreat. And gospel singers also say about their lives on tours, "When you're out here on this highway, you don't miss a thing."[6] She had an ideal background for a blues singer.

Her children, born during her teen years, had also made her mature quickly. Her career in New York and her travels to clubs around the country continued her education, ridding her of some of her remaining illusions about the world. It could be a place where people played rough and competed for political power, position, and economic gain. Her marriage to Ted White was another aspect of her early acquaintance with worldly realities.

Wexler had heard that Ted and Columbia Records executives had often had sharp differences of opinion. But Wexler never had any hassles with Ted about what to do for Aretha's career. "We got along very well," Wexler said. "Ted White never interfered with my plans and decisions."[7]

Wexler thought that Aretha and Ted were ready for guidance that was appropriate for her strengths. Preparing for her first album with Atlantic, Aretha wrote some songs and selected others. Wexler was delighted. She did her homework in Detroit, devising outlines of the songs on her piano. "I would never dream of starting tracks without Aretha at the piano; that's what made her material organic. She'd find the key, devise the rhythm pattern, and work out the background vocals with either her sisters, Carolyn and Erma, or the Sweet Inspirations"—a church-based group of singers who also were very talented and versatile.[8] Not only were Aretha's sisters talented singers, but Carolyn was a gifted songwriter, with special sensitivity for music and ideas that appealed to her generation.

Wexler took Aretha and Ted south to Muscle Shoals. Wexler had only one anxiety. He didn't want to bring Aretha to work with an all-white rhythm section and back-up musicians, so he asked Rick Hall, the man who owned the studio, to find a black horn section to play with the white rhythm section and accompany Aretha. At the time, there was a great deal of tension in the country, because of the demonstrations and violence accompanying the civil rights movement and integration. Wexler didn't want to bring Aretha down south to find "wall to wall white musicians." But Rich Hall "carelessly hired a white horn section," Wexler discovered.[9] He was relieved that Aretha didn't bat an eyelash when she saw them. She sat down at the piano and began to work. She had thoroughly professional instincts.

Drummer Roger Hawkins was thrilled when he heard her play. "I knew everything would be all right. This is not going to be any trouble at all. . . . She's really got something."[10] Above all, he loved the feeling that she put into her singing. Tom Dowd, a young, very talented recording engineer, who had just the right touch to emphasize the soulful Atlantic sound, was working in Muscle Shoals that day. "Everybody stopped in their tracks," he noticed the reaction to Aretha's first song.[11] He would often work with her in years to come. She would make fourteen albums at Atlantic with Jerry Wexler.

As time went on, she began to joke with the musicians and the others she worked with closely. She liked to tease Tom Dowd by calling him "Peck's Bad Boy." He was always ready to try something new. But the atmosphere on her first day in Muscle Shoals wasn't relaxed. The group's trumpeter, a white southerner, and Ted White began bickering. They insulted each other while drinking out of the same bottle in the studio. Wexler was worried. Aretha finished her first song, "I Never Loved a Man (The Way I Loved You)," about how her friends warned her that her man was no good. But she couldn't bring herself to leave him. She didn't know why she let him do hurtful things to her and break her heart. The musicians' earthy, funky sound gave perfect support to her groove, her steady beat. Everybody was in awe of the richness and freedom of her voice and her delivery.

The musicians in the studio also began a second tune, "Do Right Woman, Do Right Man," which Aretha wanted to sing. A taping was done with most of the rhythm section—the drums, bass, and guitar—but Aretha didn't record her vocal or piano parts for it. The lyrics were actually being written while Aretha was recording "I Never Loved a Man."

Then the day was over. Jerry Wexler went to bed at the motel where everyone was staying. Many of the others stayed up, drinking and talking—and quarreling. In the middle of the night, a fight broke out between Ted White and one of the white men. The white man had been drinking, and he called Ted White and hurled "racial invective" at him, Wexler said. Then the white man went upstairs to tackle White, and White beat him up and even held him over a balcony. The white man later told Wexler that White had been helped by "two big goons," but Wexler knew that White hadn't needed any help. When the fight broke out, the noise alerted Wexler. People ran up and down the hallway. He could hear the sound of things crashing and breaking. Doors slammed; people screamed. Wexler thought he even heard gunshots. At dawn, he went into Aretha's and Ted's room. Ted yelled at Wexler for getting Aretha and him mixed up with "all these rednecks." Tempers were out of control. Ted and Aretha left Muscle Shoals right away.

Wexler soon went to New York and provided his most important disk jockeys with acetates of "I Never Loved a Man." Sure enough, it became a hit. Everyone loved it. Disk jockeys played it constantly. Aretha, who eventually said she had no favorites—she liked all her recordings—was proud of this recording. "It was my first million seller," she would say with a quiet voice and a gleam in her eye.[12] But Wexler couldn't release a single record because he didn't have anything to put on the other side. And he couldn't find Aretha to finish the record.

For a couple of weeks he did his best to locate her. He heard a rumor that she and Ted had separated. She had been very upset by the dangerous incident in Muscle

Shoals. But she and Ted soon got back together. She walked into Wexler's office in New York, then went to prepare more songs at Wexler's house in Great Neck, Long Island—"and made a miracle," he would recall about her work on "Do Right Woman, Do Right Man." "She overdubbed. . .keyboard parts, first playing piano, the organ; she and her sisters hem-stitched the seamless background harmonies, and when she added her glorious lead vocal, the result was perfection."[13]

Aretha also had other songs ready to be recorded—"Don't Let Me Lose This Dream," "Baby Baby Baby," "Dr. Feelgood," "Save Me," and "Respect." Jerry Wexler brought the band up from Muscle Shoals to work with Aretha, including King Curtis, a funky, affecting saxophonist with a big sound, a fine tone, and rhythmic mastery.

"I Never Loved a Man" sold 250,000 copies in two weeks, rising to number nine in the pop charts, on its way to becoming a million selling hit—a platinum record—one of many gold and platinum recordings she would have. "Do Right Woman, Do Right Man" went up to number thirty-seven in the r&b poll. The next very important recording, and perhaps Aretha's best known song—the one that would become symbolic of her career and image—followed soon afterward. She and her sister Carolyn took the song "Respect," written by the starring blues performer Otis Redding, and infused it with sexiness. They added such catchy phrases as "sock it to me," which they sang forcefully and repeatedly. The public fell in love with that song, too, and gave Aretha another million selling hit, awarding her the accolade, "The Queen of Soul," to be indisputably hers alone. Earlier in the 1960s, she had shared the title with Nina Simone. In those days, she had also been billed as "The Queen of the Blues." "Respect" was released in April 1967. By June it was the number one record in the United States on the pop and r&b charts, and it was in the top ten in England, too.

Young and beautiful, with a serene expression that masked the turmoil in her private life and early recording career, Aretha took the country by storm in her mid-twenties.

"We didn't make [Aretha] a star. She was always a star. She will always be a star. We just got her into a public acceptance level," Tom Dowd would reminisce about her sudden fame in 1967.[14] "Respect" won two Grammy awards as the best r&b recording and the best by a woman for 1967 from the National Academy of Recording Arts and Sciences.

FIVE

THE GOLDEN YEARS

The hits kept coming—among them "Ain't No Way" and "Since You've Been Gone" on her first album released in February, and "Dr. Feelgood" along with "Respect" on her second album called *Aretha Arrives*. The second album itself went up to the number five spot on the charts after its release in April 1967. In July 1967, came the hit "Baby I Love You," followed by "You Make Me Feel Like a Natural Woman" and "Chain of Fools" in September. Her songs that ranked in both the pop and the r&b charts were known as crossover hits.

Though Otis Redding had written his song, "Respect," about esteem between people, Aretha directed her interpretation of the song to the sexual respect and desire that a woman wanted her man to show her. "What else does 'sock it to me' mean?" said Jerry Wexler about the line added by Aretha and her sister, Carolyn.[1] But the public, which didn't always understand every word Aretha belted, decided that she was also singing about respect in general between people. African-Americans inferred that she was singing about the respect that they were demanding from whites—and everyone else. Whites, too, who were sympathetic to the civil rights movement and other social changes, caught the spirit of the times. The message of the song became an all-encompassing directive presented in a sexy, impassioned way. Black was beautiful; black women as symbolized by Aretha's voice and presence were magnificent and formidable. So were all women. Everyone was entitled to respect. The song was so potent that it became part of the folklore of the country.

Aretha was delighted to have her recordings become hits. Now she could reap the financial awards she had been hoping for. By the end of 1967 she was winning critics' polls in *Down Beat* and *Record World* and other publications. About twenty years after "Respect" was released, *Rolling Stone* magazine would call it one of the top ten songs out of "The 100 Greatest Singles of the Last 25 Years."

Her marriage, however, did not improve. She and Ted kept fighting. Many of her songs—those she wrote and others that she chose—reflected the storminess of her married life. Everyone who worked closely with her knew about her personal problems; she had very good moods and very bad ones. But to her legions of fans she kept sending out stoic and uplifting messages with her music. Music critics concentrated on her exciting voice and technique. Poet Nikki Giovanni would one day define the revolutionary social and political impact of Aretha's music. In her "Poem For Aretha," Giovanni wrote about how Aretha pushed:

> black singers into blackness,
> Negro entertainers into negroness,
> Aretha was the riot was the leader,
> if she had said, 'come, let's do it,'
> it would have been done.[2]

Giovanni heard the revolutionary blare of Aretha's voice, not her preoccupation with her career and personal life. Aretha kept busy making records and appearing in concerts. Every place she went, she enhanced her reputation. In 1967, she traveled to England, where she was hailed as the Queen of Soul. She received a wonderful review from *The New York Times* jazz critic, John S. Wilson. He dismissed the first, Tin Pan Alley songs of her concert: "There's No Business Like Show Business," "Try a Little Tenderness," old standards, and the Al Jolson trademark, "Rock-a-Bye Your Baby with a Dixie Melody." But Wilson focused on the essence of her performance: "Miss Franklin built up slowly and with some difficulty to the triumphant climax. Her current popularity, which has been at a crest for the past six months, is based on the gospel fervor that she brings to her songs." He loved it when "she got down to business with 'Natural Woman.' Assisted by three girls who provided antiphonal responses, she coaxed, preached, belted and shouted her way through song after song."[3] The lead singer was Cissy Houston, Whitney's mother. By the end of the night, Aretha had most of the people who filled Philharmonic Hall on their feet, clapping and cheering. A jazz specialist, Wilson didn't care for the "blatantly loud orchestra." It provided a level of sound she would always like for her performances.

All the music and culture critics paid attention to her now. *The New York Times*'s George Gent called her music "deafening," but he loved her voice when he could hear it clearly. Another reviewer from *The New York Times* wrote about Aretha's second album, *Aretha Arrives*, "The rhythm and blues band. . .led by King Curtis on tenor sax produces a driving beat and a juicy, fat sound that's perfect for setting off the vocal pyrotechnics. It's held together by an aggressive, sharply rhythmic piano played by Miss Franklin."[4]

Offstage, too, she was engulfed in pyrotechnics. A writer for the *New York Post* on October 28, 1967, wrote:

> The scene in Aretha's [New York hotel] suite on her only free afternoon of the week is confusion, bordering on chaos and occasionally

slipping over the line. Ted, whose exuberance is in vivid contrast to his wife's placidity, arrives and begins making and receiving telephone calls. In between he sorts contracts. A little later, Carolyn comes in, complains about all the bills she has paid that day and breaks into her own version of a recent rock hit, singing, "And the bills go on, and the bills go on."

. . .A demonstration record hasn't arrived on time. Ted takes a good-natured complaint about the oversight and shoots back: "You'd like to see me run all the way to Detroit and get it, wouldn't you?"

Band-leader Donald Townes walks in and takes over the telephone. Carolyn examines the luxury of Aretha's suite. Her accommodations suffer by comparison and she notes this, aloud.

Aretha takes little part, finally disappears to prepare herself for a waiting photographer. In her absence, Townes, a professional for 15 years, says he has never met a performer "with such a feel for the music.". . .

Carolyn concurs: "She hears everything! Even when her back is turned." "That's A-flat!" she'll tell me, and she can barely read a note.

Aretha returns, eminently ready for a camera, the pictures are taken, and she talks a little longer. Her personal credo she sums up with the title of her most popular tune: "Respect. If you can get that, you can get the rest of it. Without it, you can't put anything together."[5]

Between February 1967 and February 1968, Aretha had six singles among the top ten pop hits and three top ten albums. Five singles and two albums sold more than half a million copies. She was surprised herself.

She told interviewers that she had thought it would take several years longer for her to become so popular. But she never said that she had doubted she would succeed.

Her shows were upbeat, hopeful, joyful demonstrations. She liked to walk to the edge of the stage to get as close as she could to audiences. One night on a tour, she tripped and fell off the edge of a stage, injuring her hand so badly that she could accompany herself with only one hand at her next recording date.

She never became involved in any offstage, purely political demonstrations. She couldn't have combined that kind of activism with her singing career. But she felt committed to the civil rights movement and other social changes afoot in the country. She had observed Dr. Martin Luther King's March on Washington and all the other activities on behalf of civil rights. She was aware of the equal opportunity acts passed in the 1960s. And she was deeply concerned and impassioned about any deprivation of rights to first class citizenship guaranteed in the Constitution. Though her own experiences on the road and so many other places had been tough, Jerry Wexler never heard Aretha utter a word against whites or any other group. But Aretha's voice, with its power, emotional impact, and gospel roots, became symbolic of the ferment and the desire and will of the people to shed their remaining shackles. With the public, she was most associated with Rev. King's philosophy of nonviolent, spiritually potent civil rights activity. Dick Gregory, who switched from being a comedian to a social commentator, would say, "You heard her all the time. You heard Reverend King only on the news. In her own way she touched people as much as any civil rights people."[6]

If people wanted Aretha to appear for a religious or civil rights related cause, all they had to do was call her father, Dick Gregory said. Her father could produce Aretha. That was true. Jerry Wexler knew that Aretha did a lot of work for Martin Luther King, Jr., and his Southern Christian Leadership Conference (SCLC). People didn't realize how much work she did for King. Wexler said, "She was acting out of the purest wellspring of faith and belief."[7]

On February 16, 1968, Aretha went to perform in Detroit, which declared it Aretha Franklin Day. Representatives for the magazines *Cash Box*, *Record World*, and *Billboard* showed up to present her formally with awards as Female Vocalist of the Year for 1967. Rev. Martin Luther King, Jr., flew in that day to give Aretha a special award from the SCLC. Rita Griffin, the managing editor of a Detroit newspaper, the *Michigan Chronicle*, told Mark Bego that she would never forget the night when Dr. King and Aretha Franklin stood on the same stage. "King had laryngitis. . . . Everybody just stood on their feet. He never said a word, because he couldn't. But you could just feel the impact his presence had. . . . At the time, people were said to be wishy-washy about King, that he wasn't militant enough. Well, all twelve thousand people in that room cared for him—you could feel it."[8]

In 1968, Aretha sang a song called "Think," that extolled the idea of freedom. The lyrics grew in force and fervor as she repeated them. She was singing about freedom in human relations. She wrote the song with Ted White, inspired by their personal relationship. But her call to freedom overrode the sexual politics and became a cry for liberty and dignity. Aretha's sound rang in people's ears.

Burt Korall, in an article for the *Saturday Review*, explained the phenomenon: "Aretha Franklin, a husky, buxom woman with a short fuse to her feelings, celebrates sensuality and womanhood in song. Following a path notable for its lack of artificiality and pretense, she moves, pushing, to the heart of the matter, vividly defining herself and the experience—stripped down to essentials. Reality is her bag; fantasy gives way as she has her say."

"With increasing emphasis in today's marketplace on truth-telling in popular song, the emergence of Miss Franklin over the past year is not without basis in the trend of things. Moreover, she is an authentic Negro artist at a time when Negro creators are heard with new ears and viewed with unrestricted interest. Popular music pacemakers no longer have to be white. The young audience, fortunately, is color blind."[9] Viewed from every possible angle, Aretha's time had come.

Less than two months after Rev. King celebrated her day with her in Detroit, he was assassinated in March 1968. Not only Aretha, but all African-Americans, and all Americans who supported the spirit of Dr. King's philosophy and work, went into profound mourning. His body was taken home to Atlanta and buried from his Baptist church there. Aretha attended the funeral and sang "Precious Lord, Take My Hand." He had often asked her to sing it for him. Around the country there were riots. The funeral procession was one of the most shockingly sad events of the decade. President John F. Kennedy had been assassinated in 1963. Soon after Rev. King died, Senator Robert F. Kennedy was gunned down in Los Angeles.

Aretha's voice helped keep the spirit of the country from foundering completely because of the violence and the loss of such good men. In June, she appeared at midnight before a crowd of twenty-one thousand people at Madison Square Garden in New York City. The show was called "Soul Together," conceived of and produced by Jerry Wexler, to raise money for the Martin Luther King Fund and the National Association of Radio and Television Announcers. "Miss Franklin turned the Garden into a 'soularium' with the heat and the light of free expression in music," wrote Robert Shelton of The New York Times on June 29, 1968.[10]

She continued the momentum of her own career with such hits as "You Send Me" and "Think" in 1968. She was such a popular figure, and soul music had become such a phenomenon, that *Time* magazine ran a cover story on her on June 28, 1968.

"In all its power, lyricism and ecstatic anguish," the magazine reported, "soul [music] is a chunky, five foot, five inch girl of 26 named Aretha Franklin. . . . She leans her head back, forehead gleaming with perspiration, features twisted by her intensity, and her voice—plangent and supple—pierces [Philharmonic] Hall:

> You make me feel, you make me feel, you make me feel like a natural woman.[11]

Time also used lyrics from others of Aretha's songs: "Dr. Feelgood," for one. He was her lover, and she didn't need any pills or anything but his loving to make her feel good. She squalled, shouted, and moaned rapturously.

The article also had some of the hallmarks of an exposé about her personal life. Ted White was depicted as an abusive husband, who hit her. Her fifty-one-year-old father was portrayed as a flamboyant minister with a "Cadillac, diamond stick pins, and $60 alligator shoes."[12] A spellbinding speaker, he persuaded people to contribute money that amounted to a handsome sum to his church, and the IRS eventually fined him twenty-five thousand dollars for not paying taxes on those contributions, estimating that his income had been more than seventy-six thousand dollars for the years 1959 to 1962. It was a great deal of money in those days. (In church circles, a minister wasn't necessarily criticized for having a taste for the good things in life. "Sure, the minister's supposed to dress good and drive good. Men of God are supposed to be fine," as one Alabaman was quoted in the book *The Gospel Sound*.[13] But that view of Rev. Franklin's proper place in his world wasn't mentioned in *Time*.)

Aretha, too, came under unflattering scrutiny. She had the musician's habit of sleeping late, then watching television in the afternoons. She deeply wanted someone

About three months after Dr. King was assassinated,
Aretha sang for a crowd of 21,000 people at Madison
Square Garden on June 28, 1968, to raise money for
the Martin Luther King Fund and the National Association
of Radio and Television Announcers.

to entertain her after she had put herself in the lonesome position of going out alone on stages to entertain others. Her habit was made to sound peculiar, though it was the ordinary way for a musician to relax and regain energy. *Time* also revealed that she smoked two packs of Kool cigarettes a day—an unhealthy habit for anyone, and certainly difficult for a singer to indulge in while performing. (Aretha would finally manage to quit smoking in 1993.) *Time* also said that she loved to cook and eat snacks. It was plain for anyone to see that the young woman, who had been slender when she had studied choreography with Cholly Atkins in 1960, had gained weight. She ate, drank, and smoked to help herself withstand the pressures of her life.

Aretha herself helped to paint a portrait of herself as a troubled woman. She told interviewers sincerely and intelligently: "Trying to grow up is hurting, you know. You make mistakes. You try to learn from them. And when you don't, it hurts even more. And I've been hurt—hurt bad."[14]

Though Aretha's main message was that she demanded respect, *Time* also honed in on some of the lyrics of "Respect" that asked her lover to take her back, to walk in the door, and to take her money in return for which she wanted him to "whip it to [her]" when he got home. *Time* also cited the lyrics from her first hit, "I Never Loved a Man (The Way I Loved You)."

Though the article mentioned that Aretha had a sense of humor, and she could mimic Hollywood actors, her brother Cecil stressed that Aretha wasn't a happy woman. "For the last few years Aretha is simply not Aretha. You see flashes of her, and then she's back in her shell." A friend said, "Aretha comes alive only when she's singing." Mahalia Jackson confided that Aretha had told her, "I'm gonna make a gospel record and tell Jesus I cannot bear these burdens alone." Mahalia opined: "I don't think she's happy. Somebody else is making her sing the blues."[15]

Aretha was hurt by the article. It was true, however, that despite her new stardom, offstage she was not very happy. At this time of her life, she was drinking too much alcohol. The difficulties in her marriage didn't help her keep her mental balance.

Mavis Staples of the gospel group, The Staple Singers, who knew the Franklin family intimately, had an opinion about Aretha's choice of Ted White for a husband: "She fooled around and got with a man like Ted White, but that's the kind of dude Aretha likes, the dude that flies fancy," James T. Jones reported in his *Vanity Fair* article.[16]

She was booked to tour in Europe again, traveling with musicians whom Ted White had hired to accompany her on the road—Detroiters led by trumpeter Donald Townes. Some also played for jazz and Motown groups. They liked Aretha's jobs most of all, because they weren't forced to follow strict rules. They could be themselves and do what they pleased. They felt camaraderie. Aretha had very friendly relations with the men and called some of them by nicknames.

Years later, some of those musicians recalled that they had respected Ted White's abilities and were grateful to him for hiring them. White was credited as the co-writer of some of her hits. Whether or not he actually wrote them with her isn't clear. Jerry Wexler thought the matter was strictly between Aretha and Ted. Her marriage to Ted, however, definitely inspired her to write some of her songs, her musicians thought. Ted's influence also inspired her to choose other hit songs she sang, even if she didn't write them. "String the titles together, and that's the story of her life," said Donald Walden, a saxophonist and one of the musicians in her group.[17] Wexler, too, thought that Aretha sang about her experiences. Among others, biographer Mark Bego reported that, at this time in her life, she said, "If a song's about something I've experienced or that could've happened to me, it's good. But if it's alien to me,

In May 1968, on a tour of Europe, Aretha had already earned the accolade "Lady Soul" in the German press, when she performed for a television program, "Aretha's in Town," in Cologne.

I couldn't lend anything to it. I look for a good lyric, a good melody, the changes [chords, harmonies]. I look for something meaningful. When I go into the studio, I put everything into it. Even the kitchen sink. I love to record. I love music. I do background vocals [for my own songs, as well as the lead vocal] because I like the sound I get when I harmonize with myself."[18]

Aboard a plane taking Aretha and Ted to Europe in 1968, Ted and Aretha fought. It was no secret that he sometimes hit her, even though he denied it. Later, a man who knew her well in this period of her life told the writer for *Vanity Fair* magazine that Aretha herself was no pussycat when she was drinking. Her musicians, who were flying in another plane, became aware of the fight. One said that Ted hit her. Nevertheless, she went on with the tour, and it was very successful.

They played at the Olympia theater in Paris, where they recorded an album of many of her hits. Jerry Wexler didn't like the album because he didn't like the big-band oriented group under Donald Townes to play for her. Wexler wanted King Curtis to lead Aretha's group. Curtis had been playing on Aretha's albums with his earthy, funky, soulful sound, with great effect and commercial success.

Aretha and her traveling band went to Juan-Les-Pins in the south of France, and to London's Royal Albert Hall, and to Frankfurt and Cologne, West Germany, and Amsterdam and Rotterdam in the Netherlands, and to Stockholm, Sweden, and Spain and Sicily. In Palermo, Italy, they played in a soccer arena during a jazz festival. Donald Walden would remember that concert as one of the highlights of the splendid trip. He walked on stage "and the audience cheered as if I was actually Aretha," he said. "I held up my hands and signaled the audience to be quiet. They became quiet. I made the peace sign, and they went crazy, cheering again. This happened several times. I went offstage and said to the other guys, 'Come on, you have to see this.'" In Holland, audiences threw flowers on stage. In Stockholm, Sweden, they threw what he thought might be glasses and salt and pepper shakers. "They were getting rather rowdy actually," he recalled. "They loved us."[19]

Returning to the United States, Aretha had prestigious engagements. She sang "The Star Spangled Banner"—a gospel impassioned, soulful version of the anthem—at the National Democratic Convention in Chicago, earning great praise from some quarters, and criticism from others. Not everyone had caught up with the times that her music reflected.

In October, she performed in Philharmonic Hall in New York City again, singing such songs as the earthy "Dr. Feelgood" and the inspiring anthem "We Shall Overcome." The audience sang, cheered, clapped, and rose to its feet. "It was a customary program of belting, soaring and volcanic vocalizing," wrote Robert Shelton, "the sort that brings chills to a listener for the absolute freedom of the voice and the intensity of passion that roils through it. On 'Ain't No Way,' Miss Franklin did some fantastic interplay with the lead singer of the seven girls who appeared with her. It brought the house down. From start to finish, Miss Franklin's performance was masterful. A large orchestra led by Donald Townes gave the star fine support."[20] An audience of forty-five hundred went to Philharmonic Hall to see her, paying $12.50 a ticket. Aretha was a superstar.

Donald Walden noticed that Aretha sometimes still seemed very unhappy, because of her personal problems, despite her success. At times she had difficulty in making herself go to the studio to record, people close to her have recalled. "But when she was ready to get up and do things, she did them," Donald Walden said. He attributed her depressions to her entire orientation as "a diva of the blues singing about the man in her life, or the man not in her life, her frustrations, her passions, all of it. That's why the music exists, as a means of expressing all the problems. Being depressed comes with the territory."[21]

Walden and others in the traveling band called her "Mona Lisa," because she had a mysterious smile. Nobody could guess what she was thinking about. Walden understood her background and her talent, and so he wasn't puzzled by her ups and downs. He had a chance to see her consistently during the good times as well as the bad. And the great times in that golden period would always be exciting for him to remember: "We had so many party-type things going on. In the Bahamas, we started having fun in a hotel suite and ended up in a swimming pool at three a.m., drinking and swimming."[22]

Musically, he loved her madly. Onstage she was absolutely reliable. "I played the introduction to 'Ain't No Way' in a real slow tempo. I was always afraid that she wasn't going to be there on time. She said, 'Don't worry about me. I'll be there when I'm supposed to be there.' Musically the most impressive thing is her depth," he would always feel.[23]

Near Denver, at the Red Rock Canyon Theater in August, an amphitheater in the mountains, the promoter had paid her only ten thousand of the twenty thousand dollars that he was supposed to. She went on stage and announced to the audience that she was ready to perform, but the promoter had not lived up to his word. And so, "I am not going to perform," she announced.[24] The audience started to throw things, Walden recalled. People set a fire and damaged a Steinway grand piano. Firemen came; the police arrived, too, and locked the musicians into a small room, where the crowd couldn't hurt them.

In Honolulu, she broke a leg on the day of a concert, which she had to postpone. Then she showed up in a wheelchair to sing for two nights. "The audience really appreciated that," Walden recalled. In Miami Beach, a group of senior citizens on a package tour from Boston, who seemed never to have heard of Aretha, went to her show at the Hotel Fountainebleau. "By the end of the set, they were dancing," Walden noticed.[25]

Walden developed favorites among her songs—
"Sweet Sweet Baby (Since You've Been Gone)" was
among them. Years after he had ceased to work for her,
he carried Atlantic's reissue of her thirty greatest hits in his
car and listened to them as he drove.

Aretha and Jerry Wexler tried to analyze her success.
In 1968, Aretha talked about her emotional appeal, saying, "I sing to the realist. People who accept it like it is. I
express problems. There are tears when it's sad and smiles
when it's happy. It seems simple to me, but for some people, I guess feelin' takes courage. When I sing, I'm saying, 'Dig it, go on and try. Ain't nobody goin' make ya.
Yeah, baby, dig me—dig me if you dare.' " With hind-
sight, years later, Aretha talked about the business side of
her music to Mark Bego: "On Columbia I cut a lot of good
stuff, and I feel that I gained an audience there. . . . I was
getting a lot of play, but not a lot of sales, and I think that
it was largely due to the kind of material that I was doing.
I was being classified as a jazz singer, and I never, ever
felt I was a jazz singer. I can sing jazz, but that was not
my forte to begin with. I think the move from Columbia to
Atlantic was about commercial success."[26]

The successful material was "an expression of the
Sixties black pride movement and her own inner feelings,"
she has also said. And she loved working with Jerry Wexler.
"My sessions [with him] are among my favorite sessions. I
feel the things we did together were dynamite, and I
would also say they were some of the finest records of the
sixties and early seventies. I enjoyed everything I did with
him."[27]

Wexler recalled: "If I had something to say that she
didn't agree with, we worked it out. There was never an
impasse or any ridicule or abrasiveness. She had superb
musicality, this gift—so unsophisticated, like a natural
child, a natural woman. There was no gloss."[28] Wexler
was also quoted as saying about Aretha: "I took her to
church, sat her down, and let her be herself."[29] He later

explained that he applied what he knew about rhythm and blues to the presentation of Aretha and didn't expect her to become a pop artist. One of the most important things he did, he reflected, was seat Aretha at the piano. She was a superb pianist for herself; she had exactly the right feeling to play in her own rhythm section.

Instead of trying to figure out what audiences might like and require her to try to please them, he presented her as she was. He invited the audiences to come to her. They came running.

* * *

In late 1968, some of the musicians then in her group recall, Ted White and Aretha split up. Ted had profited financially from the marriage. Her father was quoted in *Sweet Soul Music*, by Peter Guralnick, as commenting about Ted, "His motivation was not sincere."[30] Some musicians thought that the volatile couple's fights had prompted Atlantic to send a representative to speak to Ted about his behavior. Jerry Wexler denied that: "It absolutely never happened."[31] He didn't know exactly what had caused Aretha and Ted to decide to divorce. She had never been interested in any man other than Ted during her marriage, Donald Walden knew. At the time of her divorce, she was relying more on Wexler and herself than on Ted's ideas for the conduct of her career. The battling couple separated; this time they started divorce proceedings.

SIX

A PERSONAL COMEBACK

Unhappy though she had been during her marriage, she was also distraught by her divorce. It may have been the most difficult decision of her life up until that time. She was still, as she would always be, very close to her family, which gave her emotional support. But Jerry Wexler, for one, knew firsthand how unhappy she was about her separation from Ted White. Sometimes, late at night, she called Wexler and confided in him. Even though their relationship was primarily confined to the studios, she regarded him as a friend, and she felt comfortable talking to him about matters close to her heart. Wexler thought of her as "Our Mysterious Lady of the Sorrows." Her eyes could be dark, deep, and luminous. There seemed to be a core of silence behind them.

In the middle of 1968, she had recorded a prophetic song, "The House That Jack Built," about a woman who had everything she needed in life, except for the man who had built the fine house she lived in. Of course, Ted White hadn't built her house; she had done it herself. But the story, which she told in song, with a forceful edge to her voice, had pathos.

In 1968, she had also recorded an album, which was actually a jazz album, and it was released the next year with the title *Soul '69*. After that, a lot of time passed when Aretha didn't record anything. Atlantic had enough recordings by her already "in the can," as the industry calls records that are finished but not yet issued. So Atlantic could release even another album called *Aretha's Gold* in 1969. It included the song "The House That Jack Built," and other songs that had been her hits in 1967 and 1968. But she wasn't actually working. She was too upset. She canceled public performances, too.

For *Vanity Fair* magazine, Jerry Wexler told a story about Aretha in this period: "I remember going to sit with her at the Drake hotel and holding her hand and begging her to come to the studio because we had a room full of musicians. And finally she came in and did it. I'll tell you this. There was never any kind of attitude in the studio. Once you were there, it was beautiful."[1]

Andrew Feinman, a lawyer who handled her affairs from the early days of her career at Columbia until about 1985, was always delighted to see how well Aretha worked in the studios. She was in charge, he thought, no matter who was producing her records. She guided everybody.

But for a while her personal problems made headlines. The *Vanity Fair* article reported, "In November, 1968 [just at the time when she and Ted White separated for the last time], she was charged with reckless driving after running two cars off the road in Detroit. The next year she was arrested for disorderly conduct after allegedly swearing at and trying to slap two cops following her involvement in a minor traffic accident in Highland Park, Michigan. That same year, the Reverend C.L. Franklin allowed the Republic of New Africa, a separatist group, to hold a conference at New Bethel Baptist. There was violence. In a gun battle with police, one officer was killed. Five were injured. Franklin and his daughter were caught up at the center of the storm called the 1960s. In 1969, the *Detroit News* reported that Ted White was being sought by police for allegedly shooting business associate Charles Cook in the groin at Aretha's home. . .She was apparently drinking heavily. 'I'll tell you something about Ted White,' says Rod Hicks [a bassist who toured with Aretha for six years in the group that was hired by Ted White]. 'He didn't have no pussycat. He had a tiger on his hands when that girl got drunk.'"[2]

Aretha made herself go back to work for a new album, *This Girl's in Love with You*. She was now recording in Miami, with a group called the Dixie Flyers, plus the rhythm section from Muscle Shoals. On the album was a song, "Call Me." Aretha wrote it herself, inspired by two young lovers whom she had heard on a street. They were going in separate directions for a little while, and they found the prospect of being apart so painful that they kept calling to each other to telephone as soon as they got where they were going. One of her musicians from Muscle Shoals, who came to New York for the recording session, believed she might have had a tear in her eye as she was singing. He thought the musicians did, too. The song became a number one hit on the r&b polls and number thirteen on the pop charts.

She also did the title tune, "This Girl's in Love with You," with such feeling and finesse that it became very popular. And "Share Your Love with Me" on the album would win her a fourth Grammy award for the best r&b recording by a female for 1969. Altogether the album was a collection of songs that made fans think she was beginning to snap out of her depression. One of the reasons for her returning brightness was her friendship, which was budding into a romance and an affair, with her road manager, Ken Cunningham.

Village Voice critic David N. Bromberg praised everything about the album. First he said that "last year, Aretha the queen seemed to be a troubled, exhausted young woman whose marriage had just hit the rocks, who maybe drank overmuch, and who had to leave the circuit for a long rest and get-together. All that may be none of my business, but its relationship to this new album calls to mind the fact that music to the great artist is his breath . . .and. . .'a friend to the end.' "Her backup singers were the "summit," and "Aretha's rested and atomic voice" went "to the top on song after song. . . . Everybody at the recording sessions must have been way up for this effort. The guitar work, for example, is a dream," he said.[3]

Her personal recovery was far from complete, however. *The Amsterdam News*, the most famous New York newspaper for the African-American community, reported that Aretha had arrived in town a few days earlier in "a state of shock." The paper said the source of information was the Queen Booking Corporation. It was owned by Ruth Bowen, an agent who would remain Aretha's friend and a booking agent for several decades. The paper continued:

> Said to be "shocked" as a result of a domestic quarrel last Thursday night in Detroit with her estranged husband, Ted White, Miss Franklin was so upset that she failed to fulfill a Friday night engagement at Chicago's theatre Auditorium [Auditorium Theatre].
>
> Persuaded to go on stage Saturday night at the Kiel Auditorium in St. Louis, she appeared to be unaware of her surroundings although she was holding the microphone and the band was playing in back of her.
>
> Patrons who packed the 10,000 seat auditorium, unaware of her physical condition, started to scream and holler for the return of their money which led to a minor riot with 50 cops being

called out to prevent a more serious situation.

Informed sources told the *Amsterdam* that White, who was arrested last December for allegedly shooting a male house guest of the Atlantic record star in her Detroit home, burst into her home last Thursday and threatened violence. When her father, prominent minister Rev. C. L. Franklin, was summoned to her home by friends, he, too, was berated by White.

This so unnerved Miss Franklin that she went into hysterics. Later calmed by her staff, she attempted to make her St. Louis date, missing out entirely on two engagements in Chicago.

Miss Ruth Bowen. . .arranged for her personal physician, Dr. Aaron Wells, to hospitalize [Aretha] after she arrived from St. Louis. She also wanted it known that contrary to many unkind remarks that may have been put out about her star client, she was under a severe mental strain.

Miss Franklin recently returned to work after an eight months' layoff. Two weeks ago in Las Vegas, she concluded a successful engagement that drew standing room only audiences.

Looking slim and trim, she had been pronounced fit as a fiddle by her medic in the Motor City, who gave her the OK to resume work. But the recent entanglement with her husband from whom she's been separated for two years seemed to have brought about a strain that might keep her off the job for an undetermined period.[4]

By September, however, her next album, *Spirit in the Dark*, came out, with the title tune charged by her unquenchable spirit for singing gospel music. Aretha was holding her own as the Queen of Soul. A *New York Times* critic wondered if it was possible for her to make a bad recording. Her music was so exciting that she beat out all of her competition. The most popular song from the album was "Don't Play That Song." It wasn't Aretha's composition—Ahmet Ertegun and Benny King co-wrote it—but it was Aretha's choice. The lyrics said that she didn't want to hear a certain song, because it brought back memories—memories of Ted White, everyone thought.

Jet magazine traced her recovery during the previous year. In 1969 she had failed to show up for her scheduled performance at the International Hotel in Las Vegas. But she had tried to mend fences when she performed there in 1970. She had inspired the audience of twenty-two hundred people at the Showroom International in the International Hotel to "clap their hands and stomp their feet, to whistle and to scream. . . . A man at a stageside table was heard to bellow excitedly: 'Hey, hey, hey! Aretha's together!'"[5]

Later in 1969, she went to Europe, appearing in England, Spain, Sicily, and Italy. "In Spain, Miss Franklin performed in a bull fight stadium to more than 40,000 nearly hysterical fans who cheered her on lustily through an almost unbearable emotion-packed, soulful performance."[6] *Jet* noted that she had disappointed the audiences in Chicago and St. Louis. Tall, slender, and quiet in demeanor, Ken Cunningham, in a golfer's style cap, was shown at her side in a photo in *Jet*, as they visited the idyllic, sparkling town of Cannes on the French Riviera, enjoying a vacation.

By the next year, she had added another gold record to her collection of thirteen, with the success of her single, "Don't Play That Song." She gave a concert at New York's Philharmonic Hall, where, *New York Times* reviewer Clayton Riley said, she nearly melted the hall with her heated performance. He called her "a living tambourine."[7]

*Maturing as a glamorous folk heroine, Aretha was
described by a record producer as a "black Mae West,"
the sexy and witty old-time Hollywood actress.*

She also gave a triumphal performance at the Apollo Theater. Thousands of people showed up, and many were turned away because there were no seats available. The people who gained entrance participated "with her in an exultation of their blackness," wrote C. Gerald Fraser, an African-American reporter for *The New York Times*. "She sang soulfully—she grunted, sighed, screamed, hollered and sang." The result was what A. X. Nicholas in his book *The Poetry of Soul* called an expression of "the black man's condition. . .his frustrations, his anger, his pride—a ritual in song that we, as black people, can identify with and participate in collectively."[8]

The crowd at the Apollo shouted so loudly for her that the only way they could understand the words was to remember them from her recordings. Aretha didn't like it when reporters surrounded her after the show. She said she wasn't much of a talker, and she wanted to unwind with a little food; she had some "chicken and dumplings" waiting for her. She described her singing as "a mixture of blues and pop and a little jazz and a little funk here and there, you know, something like that. And I have to say the church had really a good deal of influence on my style, along with the experience of life in general."[9]

Aretha had told *Jet* magazine that she did not aim her music only at African-Americans. She said, "It's not cool to be Negro or Jewish or Italian or anything else. It's just cool to be alive, to be around. You don't have to be Black to have soul." She added that she did agree with writer Leroi Jones's thesis: "'Soul music is music coming out of the black spirit.' A lot of it is based on suffering and sorrow, and I don't know anyone in this country who has had more of those two devils than the Negro."[10]

Her lawyer, Andrew Feinman, like Jerry Wexler, would always remember that he never heard a word of prejudice of any kind from Aretha. Rev. Jesse Jackson heard Aretha's performance at the Apollo, along with a Zulu chief, Gatsha Buthelezi, from South Africa. And when

Aretha was introduced to the Zulu chief, one of Aretha's business associates told Feinman not to go along with Aretha. But Aretha walked over to Feinman, took him by the hand, and said, "Come on with me, don't you want to meet him?" She was unaware that he had been told to stand back because he was white and Jewish.

* * *

Aretha was back in the limelight full force. Now that she had recovered her personal balance, however, she faced the beginnings of a career crisis. Jerry Wexler had noticed that audiences were losing their ardor for soul music. The years from 1967 through 1969 had been the golden age of soul. Now Jerry knew he would have to do something to broaden Aretha's appeal. She needed to find fans among the white audiences who loved the Jefferson Airplane, the Grateful Dead, and other pop groups.

Wexler came up with a daring gamble. He would take her to San Francisco's Fillmore West, a theater that held five thousand people. The audience would consist of hippies and other white people who liked groups on the cutting edge of popular music.

Donald Townes, the trumpeter, was still leading her traveling group. As Donald Walden recalled, in 1971, Cecil Franklin, who was now managing Aretha, asked Townes for the band book that held Aretha's music. It was going to be recopied in New York for a couple of months. Townes never saw the book again. Jerry Wexler, who had always wanted saxophonist King Curtis to lead her band on the road as well as in the studio, had finally gotten his way. So Townes and the other men whom Ted White had hired were let go. King Curtis took charge when she went to perform at the Fillmore West.

Aretha was known for her brilliant and sometimes gaudy stage dresses and costumes. She loved a spectacle. For the Fillmore West, in March 1971, she dressed

In March 1971, Aretha performed with Brother Ray Charles as her special guest at a concert and on an album, Aretha Live at Fillmore West. The audience cheered and threw flowers onstage.

conservatively, but she sang with her usual fervor and abandon, playing piano for herself. Wexler was thrilled to hear the audience cheer. The performances, over a period of three nights, had cost a lot of money to produce. If the audience hadn't given its approval to Aretha, the money would have been lost. As it turned out, Aretha recalled, there was only space for five thousand people there, but about ten thousand squeezed in. Queen Booking had arranged for her to work for $20,000—more than the theater could pay. Jerry Wexler had decided to make up for the difference between the theater's payment and Aretha's required fee. Atlantic taped the concert, planning to release it as an album, *Aretha Live at Fillmore West*, in 1971.

A special guest on the album was Brother Ray Charles. After Aretha sang "Spirit in the Dark," she went offstage and came back with Ray in hand, saying, "Look who I found." They sang a reprise of the gospel-based "Spirit in the Dark." The audience, packed in and screaming, adored them. Aretha would recall her engagement at the Fillmore West fondly as one of the high points of her career. "It was just too much, loaded with soul," she said about her duet with Ray Charles. "The audience did everything. They cheered from the tabletops. They were onstage. They threw flowers onstage. It was just a night to remember."[11] She won her sixth Grammy in 1971 for the best r&b recording by a female with her single, a rocking version of "Bridge over Troubled Water," on the album. Critics called the album joyful. Jerry Wexler lauded her as a genius as great as Ray Charles.

SEVEN

A PROFESSIONAL LULL, A PERSONAL HELL

Aretha's romance with Ken Cunningham was therapeutic and anchored her life. In 1970 she recorded an album *Young, Gifted and Black*, including the song, "A Brand New Me." It was typical of Aretha to sing about what she was feeling. Though she avoided the press after the *Time* magazine article, she still sent signals about her personal life through her choice of songs. She and Ken lived together, first in an apartment on the fashionable upper east side of Manhattan, then in a six-story brownstone. She had put on weight at the end of her marriage to Ted White, but during her relationship with Ken, she slimmed down from a size fifteen, at 165 pounds, to size ten, at 125 pounds.

Mark Bego's book reported Aretha as saying that she was "feeling better now—not just physically, but also about myself—than I have in a long, long time."[1] She described the diet that she had been able to stick to. "As soon as I got up in the morning, I'd take one teaspoon of honey and two teaspoons of apple cider vinegar and stir them in about one-third glass of water."[2] She drank it before having any breakfast, and she ate very little for the rest of the day—clear soup, a dash of vegetables and fruit, and a spoonful of other foods. That was how she lost forty pounds in four months. For a woman who loved clothes, it was wonderful, she said, to be able to choose anything she wanted to wear and look good in it. She also controlled her drinking. Friends thought it was because Ken nurtured her and offered her stability.

In 1970, at the start of their six-year affair, she and Ken had a baby boy, whom they named Kecalf. Even some close friends would have trouble remembering the name, which was pronounced Kelf. It was actually an acronym—a combination of Kenneth E. Cunningham's initials first and then Aretha Louise Franklin's. Ordinarily she didn't parade her personal life to the public, but she did consent to appear on David Frost's television interview show. Preparing for it, she met with a Frost show staffer in Ruth Bowen's office and talked freely about herself and her children. Ken Cunningham stood off to the side and didn't interfere.

In his book about Aretha, Mark Bego recounted that though she had opened up and talked a lot during the rehearsal, she showed up in the studio and gave one word answers to Frost on the show. She excused herself for a minute and walked off the set to get a cigarette. And she sang several songs. Far from being upset, Frost was delighted with her naturalness; he wanted to book her again.

The album *Young, Gifted and Black* was released in 1972 and won Aretha her seventh Grammy for an r&b recording. That year, too, Aretha won her eighth Grammy for an album of gospel music called *Amazing Grace.* Jerry Wexler had been asking her to record gospel music for several years, and she finally decided to do it. Around that time, she made an appearance at a Chicago church for the funeral of the most legendary gospel singer who ever lived, Mahalia Jackson.

Miss Jackson had been a friend of the Franklin family until she and the Rev. C.L. Franklin had come to a parting of the ways. Miss Jackson liked a strict, church-oriented life. But when she died, Rev. Franklin took part in the great display of public and official mourning in Chicago. Aretha, ever the loyal daughter, went with him. People clapped for her when her name was announced at the church. It was unusual for people to clap at a funeral service. Sallie Martin, a famous gospel singer there, became very upset, and she said, "Worst thing I ever heard. . .a nightclub singer at a gospel singer's funeral."[3] But Aretha, simply dressed and beautiful, sang "Precious Lord, Take My Hand." Her voice worked itself up higher and higher, rebounding off the high walls of the church.

For her own gospel album recorded the same month that Mahalia died, she went to Rev. James Cleveland's Temple Missionary Baptist Church in Los Angeles. Ken Cunningham chose the photography used on the album cover, as he had done for *Young, Gifted and Black*. The gospel album showed Aretha in a colorful African costume and headwrap. Aretha's father delivered an emotional address to the congregation, saying he was "about to bust wide open" when he heard his daughter singing the gospel. It brought back memories for him. Aretha was taped in live performance at the church, backed by Cleveland's Southern California Community Choir. Whether she was singing gospel or rhythm and blues, she always had the good fortune to work with splendid singers in choral and backup groups.

Arif Mardin, who worked on the album with her, recalled, "It was so incredible. Aretha got extremely emotional doing some of the songs and she had to sit, you know, and kind of reflect."[4] She also recited from the Twenty-Third Psalm. For the hymn "Amazing Grace," simply the way she sang the title words demonstrated the emotion that seemed to overcome her as she sang: "Amaz—Zing—Amazing Grayaaaaaaayaaaaaaayce." It was a stunning album—and not only a Grammy winner but a great artistic and commercial success. It confirmed

Aretha's voice held the crowd spellbound when she sang "Precious Lord" for Mahalia Jackson's memorial service at McCormick Place in Chicago on February 1, 1972.

what she and her father had always contended. "I never left the church. The church went with me," she said.[5] After that album, Aretha joined the ranks of the greatest gospel singers in the country. That made her very happy. With the spirit that she had learned from Clara Ward, Aretha sang the hymn "The Day Is Past and Gone" at Clara's funeral in January 1973. She kept publicly rekindling her connection to her roots, maintaining her image as a star in the gospel world. (In the 1990s, the album went double-platinum, selling more than two million copies. She had many million selling, gold single recordings, but this was her only double-platinum album.)

Aretha kept winning Grammys for a while longer. In 1973 she won one for *Master of Eyes*, and in 1974 for *Ain't Nothing Like the Real Thing*, her tenth Grammy. The awards reflected the appreciation of the National Academy of Recording Arts and Sciences, but not necessarily the commercial successes of her records. She had some hit singles from these albums. But by the middle of the 1970s, a downturn in her career was in full swing. She knew it. Soul music had lost its cachet.

Furthermore, King Curtis was murdered in 1971, shot outside an apartment house in Manhattan. (Not only Curtis, but Donald Townes, who had preceded Curtis as leader of Aretha's traveling band, would die by violence, murdered in an incident connected with drugs.) Curtis's disappearance from her work wasn't the reason that her recordings were becoming less commercial with each passing year. But his death was emblematic of the sometimes luckless, violent landscape of her life. There were so many shocking events over which she had no control.

She produced albums with Jerry Wexler in 1974 and 1975. The album *With Everything I Feel in Me*, released in December 1974, failed to climb into the top forty on the popularity charts. That was the first time that Aretha had fallen short to that degree at Atlantic. One of the bright notes about the album was Aretha's appearance on the

Aretha holds her tenth Grammy award, which she won for her 1974 performance of Ain't Nothing Like the Real Thing, *in the category of the Best R&B Vocal, Female.*

cover. She was slender and fashionable in a white fur coat. In the late 1970s, Jerry Wexler resigned from Atlantic. Aretha kept giving high profile, public performances—on television shows such as the *Tonight Show with Johnny Carson*, the late night rock and roll show *Midnight Special*, a Muhammad Ali show, a Bob Hope special, the Grammy Awards.

But in 1975, for the first time, Aretha didn't win a Grammy. Instead, Natalie Cole, Nat "King" Cole's daughter, who idolized Aretha, began to win Grammy's every year from 1975 through 1979. Any star would feel the pain of slipping in the esteem of her peers that way. NARAS's judges were choosing someone else—a younger woman. Aretha, who was still in her thirties, was characterized in *Rolling Stone* magazine as the "aging Queen of Soul." As if that weren't bad enough, Aretha finally made some of the albums of questionable quality that a critic had once thought would be impossible for her.

Not only her career, but her domestic life became less stable. She broke off her relationship with Ken Cunningham. By January 1977, she was single again. At a charity event in Los Angeles, she found herself performing on the same bill with dancer Ben Vereen. He introduced her eldest son, Clarence, then twenty, and an aspiring songwriter, to a handsome, thirty-one-year-old actor, Glynn Turman. Turman had been working professionally for nearly twenty years on stage, in films, and on television. Among his film credits was *Cooley High*, and critics had praised his performance in "What the Winesellers Buy" at the New York Shakespeare Festival Theater at Lincoln Center in New York. He was an experienced man, with three children from two marriages. And he, too, was single, after two divorces. Clarence told him, "My mother loves you." Glynn asked who his mother was. When Clarence said, "Aretha Franklin," Glynn Turman was impressed.

She invited him to her thirty-fifth birthday party. He invited her to an acting class that he taught. The attraction between the glamorous singing star and the journeyman actor was very strong. It didn't seem to matter that she was a household word, far more famous than Glynn. In March 1978, they announced their intention to marry, and on April 11, 1978, they were married in Detroit at her father's church. Cecil escorted Aretha to the altar. She wore an elaborate silk gown with a seven-foot train. Both she and Glynn had a dozen attendants each. "The Four Tops sang the Stevie Wonder song, 'Isn't She Lovely,'" Mark Bego reported. Aretha's four sons and Glynn's three children came to the wedding. "Aretha's sister Carolyn and her cousin Brenda [who would sing in Aretha's backup groups with great success in years to come] each sang a solo at the wedding. Their wedding cake was a four tiered work of art that stood several feet tall."[6]

Her father, who performed the ceremony, offered a prayer for the success of the marriage, saying, "This couple has entered into a union which will last all their lives—hopefully." There was a curious dash of realism in the prayer.

Aretha announced that she and Glynn were lovers and best friends, even though some of their habits were poles apart. She smoked up to two packs of Kools a day. He didn't smoke. She loved all God's food. He was reported to be a vegetarian. Some people whispered that the marriage wouldn't work out. Aretha was upset enough to speak out, saying that her family and his had become one big, happy, loving group. She wanted everyone to know it.

Glynn encouraged her to try acting, while she kept recording albums that were musical and commercial disappointments. But her public appearances attracted standing-room-only audiences, and the songs she sang—often her earlier hits—were well received. *The New York Times* reviewed her concert at Carnegie Hall about two weeks before her marriage: "On her old soul hit 'Respect,' she was awesome, digging into the beat with her steamroller

On April 12, 1978, Aretha married her second
husband, actor Glynn Turman, in a ceremony at her
father's New Bethel Baptist Church. The marriage
lasted about four years.

of a midrange and pushing her band so hard that the conductor began leaping up and down out of sheer exuberance."[7] There was no doubt that she was holding onto her title as Lady Soul, the Queen of Soul. Some critics, including Robert Palmer, noted that her new material didn't have the quality of her early Atlantic hits.

She began to put back on the weight she had lost. She blamed her weight gain on her happy marriage. With seven kids to look after and feed every day, she didn't have time to worry about her figure. She was taking care of her career and her husband, too. Furthermore, she said she didn't want to go on a diet again. She had felt weak and ill often enough the last time.

And she began to wear increasingly outlandish outfits on stage. Some of them were tight, with very low necklines, and revealed her plumpness; others were simply strange to look at. One was actually a bathing suit. For a woman who loved fashion, and kept track of the newest designs from international designers, she made some odd choices when she experimented with eye-catching costumes. Too infrequently did her fancy settle on such good-looking outfits as a smart black pants suit, pretty, wide-brimmed hats, and feather boa trimming at the neckline and hips on one green dress. In her offstage, casual outfits, she often looked far more attractive and slim.

In 1979, as her contract with Atlantic was running out, she made an album—her nineteenth for Atlantic—that she hoped would recover her fortunes. She needed to become one of the popular singers who were appealing to young disco dancers. By then, disco music was the rage. But Aretha's new album failed miserably. As if her problems with criticisms of her work weren't enough to trouble her, a violent act rocked her life completely.

On June 10, 1979, her father was shot in his own house in Detroit during a robbery. Several arrests were made and reported in the national papers and wire services. Reporter Joe Swichard of the *Detroit Free Press* heard that the thieves were trying to steal one of the leaded glass windows in the minister's fine old house. The minister surprised the thieves in the act. A woman and three men were arrested in the weeks right after the shooting. But no one was ever convicted of the shooting. Rumors were passed around that the minister knew the people who shot him. Anything was possible. He had met countless people. The minister went into a coma right away and was in critical condition at Henry Ford Hospital, United Press International reported on June 23.

Carolyn Franklin received a phone call from Mavis Staples, who told her that her father had been shot and was in a Detroit hospital. Carolyn didn't believe it. She thought it was just another prank. All her life, she, along with the rest of the family, had been getting calls from people saying that their father was shot, or stabbed, or dead. Mavis Staples reminded her that their families had grown up together. She wouldn't joke about such a thing. "Call up the hospital yourself," she said. Carolyn finally decided to do it. That was how she found out that the horrific story was true. She worried that Aretha might fall apart—truly have a breakdown. But Rev. Franklin did not die. He lingered on in a vegetable state.

Aretha performed in benefits to help pay for his hospital costs. Living in Los Angeles with her husband, she traveled to Detroit twice a month to visit her unconscious father. She was preoccupied with him. He had been the most influential person in her life. Late in the summer of 1979, Aretha gave a concert at the Greek Theatre in Los Angeles. Coming out on stage for an encore, she announced, "For those of you who would like to know, my Dad is much better tonight." But he wasn't.

EIGHT

A NEW LEASE ON STARDOM

Clive Davis, who had taken over a little company called Bell Records and started Arista in 1974, believed in Aretha Franklin and in himself. He thought that all she needed to resurrect her popularity and join the trendsetters was the right material. She hadn't been singing the best songs, he knew. She missed the type of close professional relationship she had once enjoyed with Jerry Wexler.

Clive had cut a swath for himself and built a reputation at Columbia, before going to Bell and changing its name to Arista. There he continued to add luster to his reputation in the music industry by launching the careers of the young white singers Barry Manilow and Melissa Manchester. He recorded other popular artists, and he rejuvenated the lagging fortunes of African-American pop star Dionne Warwick. Dionne had originally flourished when she sang the songs of a leading songwriter, Burt Bacharach. But when they stopped collaborating, she couldn't find the right songs for herself. She wasn't working with the right producers, either. Clive Davis helped her become a star again.

Aretha studied the record ratings charts in the music industry publications—"the trades," as they're called—and decided that Clive Davis might be able to help her.

Clive Davis, president of Arista Records, felt Aretha
needed better material than she was recording in the
late 1970s at Atlantic, and he signed her to a contract
that rejuvenated her career in the 1980s.

Just before she signed a contract with Arista, she went to work in her first Hollywood movie, *The Blues Brothers*, in 1980. She had a small role as a restaurant worker whose man was a former blues band member. His old friends in the band came to the restaurant to recruit him for the band again. Aretha, in a waitress's dress, walking flat-footed in scuff slippers, came out of the kitchen to try to stop her man from leaving his job. With great strength and excitement, Aretha sang her old hit "Think," warning him about destroying their relationship. She sang the song faster than ever, and she danced energetically, too. Her man walked out with the band, but not before Aretha made it clear that, even in a dress that showed off her plumpness, she was still a commanding performer. She didn't need glittering earrings and bright furs to sparkle. Some critics thought she was the best thing in the movie.

Arista called her first album *Aretha*. It set her off in the 1980s along a path of disco songs, duets, and rock and roll. Some of her songs would be at even faster tempos than she had been singing. They were good for the disco scene, with the relentlessly regular beat and the high decibel sound that the kids liked to dance to. Her work went back on the charts. One song from *Aretha*—"Can't Turn You Loose"—was nominated for a Grammy.

Each year she would put out another album with hit singles. Clive Davis later took credit for giving Aretha special attention, collaborating with her as a virtual partner to help choose songs. He also supplied the right producers for her sessions in the studios. One producer was Arif Mardin, with whom she had worked during her glory days at Atlantic. Another was Chuck Jackson, the brother of the Rev. Jesse Jackson and a very successful producer. Chuck had co-produced Natalie Cole's Grammy-winning hits in the late 1970s. Aretha's concert career, which had seemed to falter early in 1980, regained its eminence, too. Along with other popular American stars with international

Aretha's role in The Blues Brothers *in 1980 brought her career out of a temporary lull. Some critics thought she was the most exciting person in the movie, for which she sang her old hit "Think."*

reputations, she flew to London and gave a command performance for the British royal family.

On the night of the Grammy ceremonies in New York in January 1981, she sang her nominated tune at Radio City Music Hall. Then she rushed to City Center to star in a concert, after which she was supposed to go to the forty-eighth floor of the *Time*-Life Building at Rockefeller Center to attend a party in her honor. Clive Davis and many celebrities waited for her there. When Arista had planned the party, Aretha had hinted to the publicity director that she wished he would schedule it for someplace near ground level. She didn't like heights. Nobody paid close attention to her offhand remark. On the night of the party, she made it through the Grammys, where she didn't win. Then she was nearly late for her concert, because of traffic in New York streets. At the *Time*-Life Building, she became frightened by the elevators.

She stepped into one and took it up to a higher floor. There she was confronted with another bank of elevators. She was supposed to ride from there to the party. She had already had a very exciting, exhausting night. She had been aggravated by traffic. And she couldn't stand the prospect of separating that far from the ground. She balked and went back to her hotel. Arista's publicity director later explained that she had been terrified by the movie *The Towering Inferno*, in which a tall office building had caught fire and trapped people inside. Aretha's fear made headlines and called attention to the concerts she was presenting at City Center.

For the rest of the week, the earthy woman reached heights she was more comfortable with, on the stage at City Center. The critics praised her performances. In *The New York Times*, Robert Palmer summed up everyone's opinion: "[S]he just sang magnificently."[1]

Next came her album *Love All the Hurt Away*, on which she sang a duet with the great jazz guitarist and singer George Benson. The song became very popular, and with the whole album, her most popular in six years, Aretha won over all the critics. They said she had finally merged her soulful, church-based fervor with a contemporary feeling. Actually she had always done that, but now, as the queen of soulful pop, and popular soul, she had achieved a more glamorous image than ever. "Aretha hits full, exultant stride," wrote George Kanzler, a jazz critic of the *Newark Star Ledger*.

There was talk of her performing the role of Bessie Smith in a movie about the legendary, hard-living blues singer. Bessie's voice had been so strong that it had rung out clearly in the highest balconies of theaters, even though she had often worked without microphones. Aretha read *Bessie*, a book by Chris Albertson. Then she called him—she did like to make calls herself—and told him how much she loved the book. She said the same thing to Clive Davis, who wanted to see a screenplay. But the film didn't materialize.

Neither she nor Glynn ever found a way of working together, though they looked for projects. Part of her mind was always on her father. And she focused her attention on her singing career, which was reaffirming her power over concert audiences and record buyers.

Her married life seemed settled. She and Glynn lived in a luxurious house, with pink decorations, sweeping staircases heightening the impression of grandeur, and a swimming pool, beautiful gardens, and several acres of land in Encino, California, in the San Fernando Valley. Her second son, Edward, was married in the mansion. Afterward she was hostess for his wedding dinner at the glamorous Beverly Wilshire Hotel.

Aretha was cooperating with the publicity machinery at Arista, talking to reporters, telling the world that she was a wife and mother as well as a star, and she loved to spend time with her family. About her marriage, she said, "He does his acting thing, and I do my singing thing. . .we have a lot of laughs together." She named a couple of soul food restaurants as their favorites in the area. And she said that she and Glynn went to Baptist church together. Her emotional problems were mostly in the past. "I don't drink now," she added. "Above all, I'm happy. . . . Glynn and I make TV commercials together for the NAACP."[3]

She was constantly involved in public appearances—a ribbon cutting, performances at the Roxy rock and roll club on the Sunset Strip. In January 1982, her song "Hold On, I'm Coming" from her second Arista album won a Grammy for 1981. Her next album, *Jump to It*, released in 1982, sold a half million copies, becoming a gold record—Aretha's first for Arista and the eighth gold record of her career. The title tune was very amusing, with a lot of hip talk between two girlfriends. Aretha referred to gossip about their friends as "411"—information. And she kept performing in public for high-profile events—one of them a benefit at Carnegie Hall in New York for the Joffrey Ballet, for which the First Lady, Mrs. Ronald Reagan, was the honorary national chairwoman. The *New York Post* gave Aretha the good sport of the week award for prevailing against a faulty sound system and putting across her soulful message.

Aretha had gained back all the weight that she had lost in the 1970s. She cooked wonderful food—chicken smothered in butter and rosemary, a blackout cake—and brought some of her meals to sustain her and her companions behind the scenes at public appearances. Or she ate what she found in the recording studios—such as buckets of fried chicken for herself, her producer, and everyone involved in the work. Her love for food was boundless. She couldn't bear to deny herself the tasty, rich foods she loved. She was born to be a star, not to be thin, she suggested, when she talked about her passion for cooking and eating. She wanted to write a cookbook one day. At the same time, she loved designer clothes, and she wore them even though they were conceived of for smaller women.

As late as November 1982, she told a reporter in a telephone chat that she and her husband "were doing just fine" and were planning to move to another house in California.[4] She also intended to tour the country to promote her album *Jump to It*. She was delighted about the rejuvenation of her recording career and her public performances such as a sold-out, soul music marathon at Madison Square Garden. It was scheduled to continue as an eleven-city tour. And she was tending to her father. But she confronted a problem that she couldn't resolve in her marriage at year's end.

She was more professionally secure than she had been when she married Glynn. Though he was a well-known actor, he had never achieved the international stardom that Aretha enjoyed. A family friend in Los Angeles observed that Aretha and Glynn loved each other, and they wanted the marriage to work. But "Glynn wanted a housewife, and Aretha was not about to be that," said the friend.[5] They had truly shared many things, including a passion for soul food. But when Aretha was working out of town, Glynn went out to soul food restaurants and other places where he could chat with friends. He was lonesome; Aretha's high-powered career took up too much of her time. Maurice's Snack 'n Chat on West Pico was one of his hangouts.

In 1982, at age forty, she packed and moved back to Detroit, and she claimed she was delighted to be there. She was much happier with the lifestyle there than she was in New York or Los Angeles. She was not the first diva to encounter insuperable obstacles in her marriages. Usually the men took a back seat to the high-powered careers. The arrangements turned out to be uncomfortable, unbalanced, and unworkable for everybody.

Glynn would eventually marry a woman without a show business career, and they would have a daughter and live quietly. By 1994 he had a role in a television series that had spun off from *The Cosby Show*. Aretha

Aretha sang at a soul music marathon that was sold out at Madison Square Garden, New York City, in September 1982.

would become so famous that she ascended to the status of a folk heroine in the country's popular music world. Honors streamed to her from all quarters. That was her destiny. She had been bred for it by her father, and, from her teen years on, she could not begin to contemplate a life without her career as the centerpiece. It was her obligation, she had been taught, to share her magnificent voice with the world.

NINE

DETROIT IS HOME

When Aretha moved home, Detroit was no longer the world's unchallenged capitol of the automobile world. It had become a city where the majority of people were African-American, many of whom had worked for the auto manufacturers. And the boundless optimism that had accompanied the boom time of the auto industry had disappeared. But Detroit still had vestiges of the spirit that Aretha had grown up with. The city was right in the center of the country, with none of the extremes in lifestyles and tastes of the East and West coasts. The pace of life was slower in Detroit, and people retained their affection for traditions—including traditions in music. Aretha decided she felt more comfortable in Detroit. She could see old friends, and she could be closer to her father, who still lay in a coma. To some extent, her move to Detroit was also a retreat.

From home base, she traveled to go into the studio with Luther Vandross, who produced her 1982 hit album *Jump to It*. They tried to match their success with her 1983 album *Get It Right*. Reviews were good, though sales of that album were less satisfying than those of their first album. She continued traveling to perform, too. On a flight

Aretha performed at the Beverly Hills Theater in July 1983, with her career on the upswing again, and her image more pop than soul. Her 1982 album Jump to It *had been nominated for a Grammy.*

home from Atlanta, Georgia, the weather tossed the plane around. Aretha would later remember it as tiny. The turbulence, which she called a "dipsy doodle," scared her to death. Now she was not only afraid of heights, she was terrified of flying.

Her new phobia began to give her problems. She signed a contract to take part in a play called "Sing, Mahalia, Sing," to be produced at City Center in midtown Manhattan, about Mahalia Jackson. The show was also supposed to tour in several midwestern cities, with rehearsals starting in New York in May 1984. Aretha backed out of the contract, because she was afraid to fly to New York. The show's producer sued her. Eventually a judge decided that the producer had the right to recover his production costs—about $230,000—from Aretha. The judge said she should have found another way to travel to New York, if she was afraid to fly.

Having nothing to do with her fear of flying, Aretha became involved in legal wrangling with Arista, too, about money—the handling of funds. Clive Davis would recall that he kept his distance from the problem, and he didn't think her grievances would ever came to a lawsuit. While she was trying to straighten out her relationship with the company, Aretha didn't make a record in 1984.

Her father died that year, on July 24. Aretha's sister Erma estimated that Aretha had spent over half a million dollars on him. Erma also said that Aretha couldn't bring herself to talk about her father's death, "not even to her own family. You can't even say the word death around her. You have to say passed away or find some other expression. She and my dad were very, very, very close," Mark Bego recounted in his book.[1] Even so, Aretha kept her chin up. "She handled [our] father's death very well," said Carolyn Franklin for the American Masters documentary.[2]

Aretha was very depressed by the loss of her beloved father. She had always been fascinated by France and by fashion. Her memories of Paris gave her great pleasure. So she decided to study the French language and buy a house. These pastimes seemed to have helped her through her mourning. She went shopping and found a house in Bloomfield Hills, a suburb of Detroit, and she kept her life going. But she wasn't left to tend her personal concerns completely. Legal problems continued to plague her.[3]

New York State sued her in 1985 for back taxes for recording sessions during her years at Atlantic. The suit claimed that Aretha owed forty-six thousand dollars in back taxes and fifty-six thousand dollars in interest and penalties. Her lawyer, Andrew Feinman, acknowledged that a nonresident performer must pay taxes on income earned in New York State, but the suit against Aretha was discriminatory, he said, because the State "can pick and choose who they will sue. Thousands of recording artists come to New York studios to record, and they are only enforcing the law against very few."

Aretha scheduled three concerts for Carnegie Hall for June 1985, and tickets were sold out. But she found out that she would be the target of legal action if she set foot in New York State. There would be a lien against the money she earned from the concerts. So she canceled the performances. Her brother Cecil claimed "that the cancellation was due to her fear of flying, when it may have been her fear of the New York State Income Tax Department," wrote Mark Bego.[4] The next year, the suit was settled out of court. But the cancellations added to Aretha's reputation as a star who sometimes became involved in lawsuits and backed away from her promises to perform. That was the year that Feinman, who admired and liked her very much, stopped representing her. He didn't share her views about a case she wanted to pursue, and she hired a lawyer in Detroit.

Aretha gave concerts in Detroit and Chicago in 1985, traveling by car to get to them. And when she went into a studio to make another record for Arista in 1985, she sang her vocal parts at the United Sound studio in Detroit. The instrumental tracks were done in Los Angeles and New York. The 1985 album was so successful that it made up for all the complications that had preceded its release.

During her year off, she had listened to music on the radio, deciding what she liked and what she would do for her next album.

Even before she had legal problems with Arista, Narada Michael Walden, who had played drums with the popular Mahavishnu Orchestra and then become a very successful record producer, had told Clive Davis that he wanted to work with Aretha. Davis began to pass music from Walden to Aretha. She liked it and began talking with Walden on the telephone. They developed ideas for such songs as "Freeway of Love" and "Who's Zoomin' Who?" When Aretha had differences with Arista, she and Narada stopped working. Once the problems were cleared away, they met in the studio in Detroit. She respected his musical abilities and his relaxed attitude. And they shared a passion for barbe-cued spareribs, with which they filled in the spaces between the songs.

Walden was charmed to see her arrive at the studio in a chauffeured limousine, accompanied by a security guard. She wore a fur coat over her jeans and sweatshirt. And the lyrics she helped build and then sang for her songs were slick and hip. She used a fast-paced, exciting jargon for the tune "Freeway of Love," about taking a romantic ride in a pink Cadillac. The music was backed by a heavy drum beat. She knew exactly how to handle the sexual suggestiveness of her lyrics and music. Narada told Mark Bego, "She's like the black Mae West!", refer-ring to one of the sexiest, wittiest, old-time, platinum blonde actresses ever to grace Hollywood films.[5] As always, in the studios, people found Aretha completely professional and inspirational. Another song, "Who's

Zoomin' Who?", had its roots in an expression Aretha had heard from some men in New York. They sometimes said that people were zooming them—trying to flirt and seduce them.

Aretha also sang a duet called "Sisters Are Doin' It for Themselves" with Annie Lennox, who was a member of the duo the Eurythmics. Lennox's usual partner Dave Stewart produced the track. At first Aretha resisted doing the song, because she didn't think she had time to fit it into her schedule. But she did it. Aretha liked the song, which reflected the philosophy of the feminist movement. Women were leaving their jobs as housewives and going to work, even becoming firefighters, construction workers, and traffic police. Women had never been allowed to do these jobs before. Aretha would later say about her own career: "I have always maintained a real man is not going to be intimidated by me. Some can rise to the occasion, and others cannot."[6] She spoke with a quiet, formal air of resolve, and with a little Mona Lisa smile playing at the corners of her lips, for the American Masters documentary.

"Sisters Are Doing It for Themselves" turned out to be a very popular song. Aretha took a lot of the credit for producing the whole album, which artfully blended her soulfulness and rock-and-roll mastery. She explained that it had taken her time to become experienced enough about the technical aspects of recording, but now she was even thinking about producing albums for other artists. The album was named for the song, Who's Zoomin' Who?

On her first video, released the same year, the song "Freeway of Love" was enhanced by a pink Cadillac with tail fins. Aretha wore her hair very short for the video. From time to time she adopted that hairstyle, which was very chic and flattering for her. The video allowed her fans to see her in performance without her having to leave Detroit.

The album Who's Zoomin' Who? contained five hit songs and sold so well that it became her first Arista album to go platinum—to sell more than a million copies. (Only

Brought together by Clive Davis, producer Narada Michael Walden and Aretha began developing ideas for such songs as "Freeway of Love" and "Who's Zoomin' Who?" in the mid-1980s. At the 1986 Grammy awards, she won a Grammy for "Freeway," and her album Who's Zoomin' Who? became her first Arista album to go platinum—to sell more than a million copies.

her Atlantic album *Amazing Grace* had outsold it.) "Freeway of Love" became the most popular song on the album, rising to number one on the r&b chart and number three on the pop chart, and it also went to number one on the dance music chart. The song "Who's Zoomin' Who?" ran a close second. The album affirmed the total rejuvenation of her career. Many younger, slimmer singers had challenged her, but she had prevailed as the "Queen of Soul."

In Michigan, the state government declared that May 23, 1985, was Aretha Franklin Appreciation Day. Her voice was officially declared "a natural resource." In July, a section of Washington Boulevard at State Street in Detroit was renamed Aretha Franklin's Freeway of Love. And in August, part of Linwood Boulevard, on which stood the New Bethel Baptist Church, was renamed C.L. Franklin Boulevard.

Mark Bego, interviewing her in 1985, asked if she had any romance in her life. "Oh, absolutely, absolutely. What would life be without romance?"[7] She wouldn't say who her boyfriend was. Bego discovered on his own that he was Willie Wilkerson, a former Detroit fireman. Aretha would involve him in the mechanics of her career, so that he shouldered some of the responsibilities for her group when it went on the road again.

At the 1986 Grammy awards, she won a Grammy for "Freeway of Love." She also sang for Coca-Cola and Dial soap commercials done in Detroit, so that she didn't have to leave town. She admitted that her fear of flying had cost her the opportunity to sing at the Kennedy Center in Washington, D.C., when Lena Horne was honored in 1984. And Aretha couldn't appear for Rev. Jesse Jackson at the Democratic Convention in 1984. "But look out—the girl is coming," she told Mark Bego in 1985.[8]

She made a series of commitments to appear in concerts—one of them at Radio City Music Hall in New York, where tickets were sold out. She canceled that date and gave concerts only in the Midwest, at halls only a few hours from her house. Even her first television special, called "Aretha!" was taped in Detroit. For this, she sang some of her Columbia, Atlantic, and Arista hits. On gospel songs, her sister Carolyn and brother Cecil joined her with a large choir. She also took part in another television special starring the Temptations and the Four Tops in the summer of 1986. That, too, was taped in Detroit. If Aretha wouldn't go to the entertainment industry, the entertainment industry would go to Aretha. She was enough of a star to demand that kind of attention and respect, when she didn't have her spirits up enough to leave town. Her idiosyncratic reluctance to travel even seemed to give her a mysterious aura that added to her charismatic appeal. She was a true winner again. She endured criticism for her low-cut gowns for her own television special, but nothing could diminish the respect that people felt for the authority of her soulful voice.

In January 1987, to entice her to perform in a television special, "A Soul Session: James Brown and Friends," the taping was scheduled for Detroit, at the Club Taboo. Aretha, who was a part-owner, felt right at home. James Brown, the "Godfather of Soul," had never sung with Aretha before. The audience never knew how strongly the two stars clashed behind the scenes—because of professional competition for the limelight, said some observers. Aretha loved the adulation that the audience in Detroit gave her during her public taping there.

For her next album, which was called *Aretha*, as her first Arista album was, she recorded the song, "Jumpin' Jack Flash," originally a hit for the rock group the Rolling Stones. Aretha's version was used as the title track for a film starring the newly famous actress and comedian Whoopi Goldberg. The song had a life of its own on the pop and r&b charts. And, for her album, her duet of the song called "I Knew You Were Waiting for Me," with George Michael, a young pop star, brought her to the attention of a young audience. In return, she gave Michael a touch of glory for singing with her. Not only did that song go to the number one spot on the pop chart, but the album was certified gold.

In 1987, too, she was the first woman to be named to the Rock and Roll Hall of Fame. Because she still wouldn't travel, Cecil went to pick up the citation for her at a formal party at the Waldorf Astoria Hotel in New York. Honored along with Aretha was Ray Charles, among other legends in soul and rock and roll.

In 1988, she won Grammys—one for her duet with George Michael, another for the album Aretha. Instead of devising a way to go to the Grammy ceremony without flying, she sat home and watched the show on television, with her boyfriend. They feasted on snacks—beans and corn bread, she said—in her white, six-bedroom, colonial-style house on three acres of land with a swimming pool and gardens where she grew her own vegetables and flowers. Cecil went to pick up her award, just as Jerry Wexler had done during her early days at Atlantic, before the ceremonies became lavish, televised affairs.

For her next album, which she produced, *One Lord, One Faith, One Baptism*, she simply went virtually next door, from Bloomfield Hills to her father's church in Detroit, to record. It was an ambitious project. Rev. Jesse Jackson took part, and so did Aretha's sisters Carolyn and Erma. Aretha did a duet with Mavis Staples at the church for the album, then asked Mavis to go to a studio and redo the hymn. Mavis thought the original version, on which she was singing lead, was fine, but Aretha never was satisfied with it. Mavis would tell the writer for *Vanity Fair* that Aretha had been competitive about that duet. In any case, Aretha had the clout to do what she wanted—stay in Detroit and conduct a high-powered career. Technology was her handmaiden.

The honors for her singing kept outweighing the criticisms. In 1988 the NAACP gave her an award as the female Artist of the Year. She won a Grammy for the album

124

One Lord, One Faith, One Baptism, though it never became as popular or commercially successful as her previous gospel album. Some of her previous mentors and collaborators—Jerry Wexler for one—marveled at how well she had rebounded from her career slump.

TEN

HOLDING ON TO
DREAMS AND RESPECT

One Lord, One Faith, One Baptism was the last album on which Aretha worked with her pretty, slender sister Carolyn. For the film *The Blues Brothers*, Carolyn had been one of the perky, girlish singers and dancers in Aretha's group. Now Carolyn was diagnosed with cancer. She and Aretha had spent so much of their lives working and laughing together. Carolyn could have launched a singing career on her own—perhaps. She had the voice and the talent, but she also had other strong interests, and neither she nor Erma had Aretha's drive or commitment about a singing career. Aretha was the leader. Yet in her own way she leaned on Carolyn as much as Carolyn leaned on her. Their combined ideas made "Respect" the great hit it was. It gave Aretha exactly the boost she needed early in her career. Carolyn also wrote material for Aretha—"Gotta Find Me An Angel" and "Ain't No Way," to name just a couple of the big hits. And Carolyn was also a talented arranger.

In 1987 Carolyn had a major operation. Then Aretha took her to the house in Bloomfield Hills to recuperate. Though she was in her forties, Carolyn had been working on a college degree, with the idea that she would

126

go on to law school. She wanted to practice entertainment law and try to help young people entering the music world. She had seen many of her sister's problems with the business side of her career. She had also seen other young singers encounter insuperable problems. She didn't want to give up the goal of her law degree even though she was sick.

While Carolyn was struggling with cancer, Aretha kept busy with projects in Detroit. She sometimes broke engagements for appearances on television even though she was in town. No one was ever absolutely certain that she would show up. In April 1988, sick in bed, Carolyn was awarded her college diploma from Marygrove College. Her sister Erma said, "Carolyn was so proud, she slept with her diploma."[1] Ten days later, Carolyn died. She was buried from the New Bethel Baptist Church. Once a source of happiness and triumph for Aretha, it was now the scene of too many heartbreaking family funerals. Her beloved relatives were dying young.

In this period, Aretha sat for interviews for the filming of the documentary in the American Masters series. Film clips of Carolyn were also used. Aretha said very little about her personal life. Even so, the documentary was fascinating. In her public life, Aretha had been a part of many important historic events. She did not have to delve deeply into her private griefs to make her life story touching. (A radical, controversial New York City public school assistant principal, who was not mentioned in the documentary, provided insight about the inspiration she gave others. He invented a fantastic plan for what he thought should be a typical day in school for African-American students. One of the elements would be "loudspeakers. . .[that] continuously bathe [a student] with the quiet sound of Malcolm X speaking, LeRoi Jones reading one of his poems, Aretha Franklin singing a soul song."[2]

Other people in the documentary, however, talked about her father, her mother, her brothers and sisters, Ted

White, and many of the tensions, losses, and victories in her private and professional life. Simply the mention of her sorrows contrasted affectingly with her poised, restrained demeanor. Clearly Aretha's experiences would have crushed a weaker spirit. Twenty years earlier, *Time* magazine reported that Aretha had said to Mahalia Jackson, "I'm gonna make a gospel record and tell Jesus I cannot bear these burdens alone."[3] Now that sentiment made sense to everyone. Yet Aretha seemed more sure of herself than ever.

Some viewers were dissatisfied with the documentary, for the very reason that Aretha spoke in a measured way. Reviewing the documentary in *The New York Times*, critic Jon Pareles remarked that Aretha "smilingly gives nothing away. . . . Only her performances reveal the passion that made her the queen of soul." Pareles also derided Aretha's development into a pop artist at Arista. "She is shown [in one of the many performance clips that peppered the documentary] singing her first Arista hit, 'Jump to It'—a song about dropping everything for a man—in bleached blond hair, blue eye shadow and a peculiar dress with a kind of pontoon hanging off one shoulder."[4] He preferred film clips from a "less guarded 1967 interview" that she gave to the press, when her speaking voice was high and innocent.

The show did, however, reveal Aretha talking about those elements of her life that she thought were important—among them her close relationship to her father, her pride in her children, her reverence for her gospel roots, her enthusiasm for future songs she would sing, and her steely belief in her position as the "Queen of Soul." These—and the privacy that she tried to maintain by commenting so little on the grittier problems she had faced—represented her enduring values and her longing for positive experiences.

A viewer would have to do private research to discover that her son Clarence had written a song she recorded.

128

By the 1990s, Edward would become a theology student. Teddy, Jr., who played guitar, would travel with his mother's groups. The youngest, Kecalf, also musical, was maturing at a time when his generation was developing rap. That's what he loved. Aretha also refrained from mentioning that Clarence was mentally ill—a "schizophrenic," the *Vanity Fair* writer said.[5] A friend in Detroit added that Clarence suffered from fantasies about himself and Elvis Presley. The "Queen of Soul" simply could not bring herself to tell her fans about all her troubles. The lessons she had learned were her own, and one of them was to keep her guard up. She felt she had a right to hide whatever she wanted to.

Aretha kept doing recordings, and a commercial, and she sang the theme song for the NBC television series *A Different World*. Instead of becoming more of a recluse after her sister's death, Aretha decided to leave town for the first time in several years. It was Aretha's way of keeping her life going and her spirits up. She had a luxurious bus built for her, and off she went, with more than twenty people, to perform at Trump's Castle in Atlantic City. With her went people in her stage group, and a hairdresser, a dresser, and road assistants. She took along a glamorous wardrobe with spangles and sequins. She always knew how to get all eyes trained upon her. And she sported a short, reddish-blonde hairstyle. Afterward, she headed right back to Detroit.

From then on, she continued to travel. In the 1990s, she would be sighted all around the country, even in New England, giving concerts to cheering audiences, and feeling proud of herself. "They loved us," she frequently said firmly about her concerts. She would make an exciting guest appearance, playing piano and singing, with Candice Bergen, on *Murphy Brown*, a television comedy series.

Reviews of her albums and performances always had something fine to say about her. *Rolling Stone* thought the duets and the songs she sang on her 1989 Arista album, called *Through the Storm*, were disappointing, but the album

Aretha's voice won rave reviews as one of the glories of American music when she appeared at Radio City Music Hall in July 1989.

reached a high point with the remake of her old hit "Think." *The New York Times* reviewer loved Aretha's duet with young, soulful singing star Whitney Houston, the daughter of Aretha's former backup singer Cissy Houston of the Sweet Inspirations. *Daily News* writer David Hinckley liked the duet that paired queen Aretha with princess Whitney, too. The title tune done with Elton John was a top twenty hit. A duet, "Gimme Your Love," was done with James Brown.

Sounding "firm and confident" to Hinckley in conversation by phone, Aretha said she was going back to Atlantic City in 1989, and she was looking forward to a concert at Radio City Music Hall. She had a lively interest in discussing her career and the music business in general: "As for getting into the Rock and Roll Hall of Fame, I have to say I never thought of myself as a rock 'n roll singer. But as they deal with people who are regarded as legendary or classic, it was certainly nice to be included. The question of what kind of singer I am is interesting. Sometimes I think of myself as pop or r&b. But mostly I'm just a singer. That spans the whole realm of music."[6]

On July 8, 1989, she opened a three-night engagement at Radio City, with its capacity for an enormous crowd, and won a rave review in *The New York Times*:

> Aretha's voice is one of the glories of American music. Lithe and sultry, assertive and caressing, knowing and luxuriant, her singing melts down any divisions between gospel, soul, jazz and rock, bringing an improvisatory spirit even to the most cut-and-dried pop material. Her concert. . . presented the singer as a glitter-swathed supper club entertainer.[7]

And as reviewers would do from time to time, taking liberties to make their columns entertaining as well as filled with details, Jon Pareles mentioned in *The Times* Aretha's odder choices for stage costumes. At one point, she walked onstage "in a yellow robe that looked like a piece of camping equipment; at the end, she donned a glittery pink, fur-trimmed robe, complete with train."[8]

To underscore her position among the luminaries of the world, particularly African-American celebrities, Aretha presented a slide show including her meetings with Rev. Jesse Jackson. She sang ballads and her classic hits in a show meant to gather new fans and keep her old ones happy. Nobody got tired of hearing her sing her classic hits. She was cannily promoting herself as a legend.

"Trim, beautiful and sexy" at age forty-seven, wrote *New York Post* critic Ira Robbins, Aretha Franklin sang with a voice that is "one of the world's truly great singing voices: a miracle of power, range, richness and subtlety that she controls like a virtuoso."[9] David Hinckley described her entrance for her opening at Radio City Music Hall with the usual attention critics paid to Aretha's production ideas: "Aretha Franklin returned to New York with grace and style . . .specifically she arrived on the stage of Radio City in a pink Cadillac filled with pink balloons, and stepped out wearing a floor-length sequin dress in ice blue, draped in a bright yellow duster lined with blue ostrich feathers. Somewhere Liberace [a pianist known for his elaborate clothes and candelabra on the piano] was smiling. . .she still sounded like no one else, too, rich and full in the middle of her range."[10] He knew that she was fighting a cold; that was why she didn't sing as many high notes as usual.

Her career had reached a plateau on a very high plane. *People* magazine ran a story on her old house on Sorrento Street in Detroit. She still owned it; it was unoccupied, and it had become run-down. The neighbors were complaining about it. Perhaps Aretha had let that happen, David Hinckley wrote in the *Daily News*, just so people wouldn't get the idea that things were going too smoothly for her. The house remained in the same condition for years more to come.

Actually, in her private life, in 1989, Aretha suffered another shocking loss. Her brother Cecil, a few years older than she, died suddenly from a heart attack. One businessman in New York who liked to wake up and get work done early in the day had sometimes been irritated by Cecil as Aretha's manager. Cecil slept until midday. He kept the same hours as his sister. But the businessman could never understand how Cecil could turn down the sound on his phone, sleep, and ignore business until noon. But Cecil had to consult Aretha during *her* hours. They had worked together very well. Suddenly he was gone. Once again, Aretha went to the New Bethel Baptist church for a sorrowful family funeral.

Afterward, she rarely went to that church. Rev. Robert Smith, Jr., who replaced her father as pastor of the church, told *Vanity Fair*, "I think that when she enters now she gets a feeling of bereavement. It's hard for her to be in here and not think of what's happened to her family. You look in her eyes and you see sorrow."[11]

Her half-brother Vaughn, who retired from the service, began traveling with her. Returning to Radio City in 1989, Aretha had another triumph, although this time Jon Pareles found the big, overly ornamental orchestra behind her distasteful. Aretha didn't like the mistakes she heard from the musicians and told them on stage, "With those mistakes that I heard, it's going to be a trio next time." Pareles wished she was serious and would hire only a small group so that everyone could hear that "her voice is still strong, agile, unpredictable and moving in all its subtleties; even in second-rate material she turns a song into drama that's both compelling and playful." Pareles remarked that her green gown made her look like "an ambulatory salad," but his review began with praise for her singing and piano playing—even though she had a cold. The crowd rose to its feet for her song "Dr. Feelgood." "For the length of the song, earthy and divine passion were inseparable, as they were when Ms. Franklin ruled soul music in the 1960s."[12]

Aretha didn't have to worry about new material anymore. *People* loved to keep hearing the music that had made her a legend. They even liked to see her adorned in all the idiosyncratic finery that she could concoct. Her terrible taste in clothes was an endearing foible. She went traveling as usual in her custom-made motor home. It was equipped with videos, stereo equipment, a caterer, and other comforts and amenities, Aretha told Florence Anthony for the *New York Post*'s Page Six in August. Aretha also said she was going to view several designer fashion shows, and she planned to design her own wardrobe the following year. She spoke of recording new songs, and she was contemplating two television shows—one a weekly variety hour, the other a situation comedy with a gospel theme. She was inspired, she said, by the success of television talk show host Arsenio Hall. At an earlier time, she had used him to open for her show after she saw him work for singer Gladys Knight in Atlantic City.

She went to Atlantic City again in her motor home that year, headed to New York to entertain at the Waldorf Astoria, where she sang a song with her son Edward, and then she returned to New York again to collect a 1990 Grammy Legends Awards from NARAS on December 5. Also honored were country singer Johnny Cash; soulful pop singer, pianist, and songwriter Billy Joel; and producer-arranger Quincy Jones, all of whom had many Grammys, with Jones leading with nineteen. Aretha was in second place with fifteen.

She still wasn't flying out of the country or anywhere else, and she occasionally canceled a planned engagement. But with her relentless drive, she managed to keep herself in the public eye. It was remarkable how her involvement in music buoyed her through her grief. She showed up to honor South Africa's leader, freedom fighter Nelson Mandela, during his visit to Detroit in 1990, soon after his release from prison. She entertained at events such as the Congress of Racial Equality's sold-out annual awards in January 1991, at the Sheraton Centre. All the while, she affirmed that she had found her musical niche, repeating her greatest hits and interspersing them with other material.

For her appearance at Radio City in September 1991, she gave a writer from *The New York Times* a chance to comment on her arrival onstage "in a ruffled red dress that made her appear trapped inside a Valentine's Day candy box." Later she modeled an unflattering yellow dress that was designed, she said, by Arnold Scaasi. At the end of the evening, "she came out in outlandish scarlet finery that made her resemble a float in the Rose Bowl parade."[13] The performance of "A Natural Woman" was also accompanied by a slide show of fashion photos of her posing in various gowns and hairstyles. And even though the reviewer didn't like her musical performance that night, it didn't matter one bit to Aretha. She knew how to mount a spectacle. No one could hurt her career anymore. The critics' remarks about her clothes actually let them join in her fun and contribute to her status as a legend.

That year, she dedicated a new album, *What You See Is What You Sweat*, to Carolyn and Cecil. She showed up in February 1992, to accept a Lifetime Achievement Award from *Billboard* magazine, nearly causing a riot. *People* jockeyed for position to watch her arrive dressed in a turquoise and lavender Chanel suit at the Laura Belle restaurant.

She was included in the trend for recording companies to put out collections of the work of the most important artists. Atlantic had released *Aretha Franklin's 30 Greatest Hits* in 1986; then, in 1992, *Aretha Franklin: Queen of Soul*, with eighty-six songs she had recorded between 1967 and 1976. Sony released thirty-nine songs done by Aretha for Columbia during the 1960s—also a musically brilliant collection. If she had been unfocused in those years, it no longer mattered. The collection demonstrated that nothing became a legend more than her ability to sing everything as well as or better than anybody.

Gary Giddins, the renowned jazz critic for the *Village Voice*, in his Weather Bird column on October 13,

1992, described the Atlantic reissue, *Aretha Franklin, Queen of Soul*, as "the most original body of singing to come out of pop or jazz in the 1960s."[14] The bins in the music stores were filled with all sorts of recordings by Aretha, including her Arista albums.

Instinctively, and perhaps from habit, she still played cat and mouse with the press, granting few interviews. The *New York Post* printed a story on November 25, 1992, about Aretha and the Internal Revenue Service. The tax agency of the federal government had placed a lien on her Bloomfield Hills house so that she couldn't sell it. The house was estimated to be worth about $2 million, and she supposedly owed the government $250,000 in back taxes. An unnamed source of information who was said to be close to Aretha told the *Post*: "[The government] doesn't have to worry. . . . She'll never sell. Aretha told me that was her dream house."[15]

The house had white carpeting, cabinets, and furniture, friends said, and one added, "There are gold cages with birds in them all over, a swimming pool, tennis court and several garages for Aretha's blue Rolls Royce and Excalibur. Plus, she has her Queen of Soul robe and crown displayed in two separate glass cases."[16] The *New York Post* article mentioned her earlier New York State tax problems and suggested that Aretha missed the help her brother Cecil may have given her in managing her money.

Aretha was in the gossip columns again on December 30, reported to have caught the wedding bouquet tossed by her niece, Sabrina Garrett, at her wedding on December 19 in Detroit. Aretha's bodyguard caught the tossed garter. The *Post* reported: "A source tells us, 'I don't know his name, but Aretha lifted up her dress and he slid the garter up as far as he could. Then she headed to the corner of the room and tugged it up over her thigh. The two of them mysteriously disappeared after that.'"[17]

Because the gossip columns are known for sometimes blending information with entertainment, and promoting careers, it's possible that Aretha might have realized that this item would be placed in the newspaper. The news could tantalize her fans and still allow her to keep secrets about her private life. She liked to tell people she was an ordinary woman. "I'm just like anyone else, just like my neighbor," she said often. "I go shopping in the supermarket, and one day the fruit is good, and one day it isn't too good."[18] She had a vision of herself as a woman who loved her home life and preferred to stay out of the public eye when she wasn't performing.

But she had won more Grammys by 1993 than any other female singer except for Leontyne Price, who had retired from the Metropolitan Opera in the 1980s. Even the great jazz singer Ella Fitzgerald won a couple fewer Grammys than Aretha. And Aretha, who had a privileged view from the top of a pyramid, had acquired exceptionally good perspective on what she could neglect and bypass, and what she had to do in the best interests of her career. She knew how to dart in and out of the public eye, reappearing now and then to remind audiences that she was the queen.

In early spring 1993, she arrived in New York, with a calm, level look in her eyes, and she rehearsed tirelessly in a midtown recording studio for several performances. The first took place at the Nederlander Theater in the Broadway district. Aretha was surrounded by singing stars— Bonnie Raitt, her old friend Smokey Robinson, Rod Stewart, Elton John, Gloria Estefan, and P. M. Dawn—to raise funds with a benefit concert for the Gay Men's Health Crisis for AIDS. Actors Dustin Hoffman and Robert DeNiro also appeared with her. Called "Aretha Franklin: Duets," the show gave her the chance to sing every style of music. Although her voice was lower and huskier than it had been in her youth—all singers' voices get lower with age—she outsang all her duet partners "so thoroughly they could only hope for a quick and merciful conclusion," wrote critic Jon Pareles in The New York Times.[19] Don

Aretha starred at the Nederlander Theater in a show called "Aretha Franklin: Duets," an AIDS benefit concert, on April 28, 1993. Standing behind Aretha is her old friend singer Smokey Robinson. On his left, from left to right, are singers Gloria Estefan, Rod Stewart, Bonnie Raitt, and actors Dustin Hoffman and Robert DeNiro. New York Times critic Jon Pareles praised her for outsinging all her duet partners.

Aquilante in the *New York Post* mentioned, as everyone else did, that Aretha made one entrance for the show in a ballet costume and tried to pirouette. It was one of her nuttier production numbers. She also sang a duet with the powerfully built, platinum-blond singer Rod Stewart, who couldn't take his eyes off her low-cut gown. She enjoyed his reaction and flirted with him. The concert was taped to be aired on television in May.

She was also honored that spring at the *Essence* magazine awards at the Paramount Theatre, along with singers Lena Horne, Tina Turner, and Senator Carol Moseley Braun, the first African-American woman to serve in the U.S. Senate. Then Aretha spent a couple of nights performing at Radio City Music Hall, where she joked about her own attempts at ballet at the Nederlander. During this visit to New York, she was promoting her son, Kecalf, as a rap artist. "He's really good," she told Sheila Rule for *The New York Times*. "We've sent his work out to various labels, and many are listening and evaluating. He performed at my birthday party, and he's been rocking the house lately."[20]

She also said that she wanted to write her autobiography and would pick a writer to help her by the fall. In 1985 she had also discussed writing a book about her life, but when she was offered a little more than half a million dollars as an advance from Doubleday, a very big publisher, she had turned it down. She wanted four times as much money, it was reported in the papers, and most of all she didn't want to write the whole story. She might concentrate on the years she had spent traveling with her father's gospel caravan and perhaps include her own poetry. The fall of 1993 came and went without her choosing a writer to work with her. Ruth Bowen, the booking agent, who had been Aretha's friend for decades, knew that Aretha still wanted to keep her secrets. Asked by one prospective, hopeful writer if she would ever talk about Ted White, Aretha said, "I think I'll skip that."[21]

She remained the elusive Mona Lisa of American popular music, emerging from her Detroit retreat to collect awards, among them honorary doctorates, and the Kennedy Center Honors Award for 1993. She sang "I Dreamed a Dream" for President Bill Clinton's inaugural and performed at other White House events. She joined the "parade of stars" for the United Negro College Fund telethon. In February 1994, she was VH1's Artist of the Month.

Then she won her sixteenth Grammy—a Lifetime Achievement Award from NARAS—in March 1994. She had also been nominated for a Grammy for singing "Someday We'll All Be Free" for the soundtrack of the movie *Malcolm X*. Appearing onstage at the Grammy ceremonies in a stunning white, low-cut gown with long, matching cape that covered her infamous decolletage and made her look regal, she thanked some people connected with her career from its earliest days. One, of course, was her brother Cecil. Then she was overcome by emotion at his memory. She turned her head aside and looked back over her shoulder. When she faced the audience again, she appeared as composed as the Sphinx. Jerry Wexler, who was watching the show in his house in Florida, later learned that she actually had felt flustered by time constraints. Not long before her appearance on the show, singer Frank Sinatra, accepting his Lifetime Achievement Grammy, was cut off by an advertisement. Aretha onstage asked the network not to cut her off. Fumbling with papers, she overlooked one piece with the names of John Hammond, Jerry Wexler, and Clive Davis. Right after the show, realizing her bizarre oversight, she began to cry.

Vanity Fair published a fascinating profile of Aretha that month, recapitulating her life and adding up the hits: "fifty eight albums, with seventeen top Ten singles (more than any other female singer in pop history)." Shedding light on Aretha's mature opinion of herself, writer Jones recalled columnist Liz Smith's criticism of a very low-cut dress that Aretha had worn at the Nederlander Theatre:

In 1986, Aretha appeared on the American Music Awards telecast. Her segment was broadcast live from Detroit. She won awards for Favorite Soul/R&B Video, Female, and Favorite Soul/R&B Single, Female, for the video and song "Freeway of Love."

"She must know she's too bosomy to wear such clothing, but clearly she just doesn't care what we think, and that attitude is what separates mere stars from true divas."[22]

Ignoring the compliment to her diva-hood, Aretha retorted in a letter to Smith, "How dare you be so presumptuous as to presume you could know my attitudes with respect to anything other than music. . . . Obviously I have enough of what it takes to wear a bustier and I haven't had any complaints. When you get to be a noted and respected fashion editor, please let us all know. . . . You are hardly in a position to determine what separates stars from divas since you are neither one or an authority on one, either." Jones commented, "Well, nobody said she'd mellowed."[23]

Jones met her for an interview at a Detroit restaurant, where she greeted him by saying:

> "You probably thought we'd never get together."
> She had canceled and rescheduled the interview many times. Jones joked about it with her and later wrote, "I didn't take [the cancellations] personally. Aretha gets cold feet. She cancels things, gets nervous, procrastinates. Like lightning, Franklin sparks at random. You never know what's going to happen. And you never know whether she's making you wait because she's the queen or because some part of her is scared, suspicious. Brilliant or 'no show,' regally temperamental or extremely terrified, Aretha doesn't flounder between the extremes. She's on or off, up or down, and you sense that this is something she cannot consciously control."
> She toyed with a taco salad and went on to filet mignon, gently reminiscing just a little about her mother and the talented musicians who had grown up in her neighborhood.

When asked about how people at the New Bethel Baptist Church reacted to her first pregnancy, Aretha bristled. "'I'll talk about that in my book,' she says firmly; she keeps her secrets. . . Carolyn King, a former New Bethel secretary who sang backup for Aretha, says, 'She'll only let you ask her so much. . .sometimes you want to know a little bit more, but some things are between her and God.' To Aretha, even in a tell-all age, there is dignity in silence."[25]

For the primary photograph to illustrate the story, Aretha reclined on an elegant couch, wearing a very low-cut black dress. A small heart, which looked gold and bejeweled, dangled from a chain around her neck. With her eyes closed and one well-manicured hand pressed against her oft-featured bosom, Aretha looked extremely seductive.

Talking with Jones, she averted her eyes, which brimmed with tears, he said, when he asked her about her father. (One of her friends told Jones: "You go in her house, you're going to see this room which is a shrine to her father with pictures of him and candles. And you're going to see this big Lucite box right at the door. . .with this big rhinestone crown in it.")

Her single status was on her mind, and she mentioned her fine opinion of herself, finishing with the idea: "The brother that gets me is going to get one hell of a fabulous woman." She said she liked simple things about men. "Nothing. . .that's unrealistic or impossible. My standards are not so high that this person is not real."[26] She went to buy doughnuts, then returned to Jones: "One thing I want to add. The best ones are married. . . .You know, when I was in the dressing rooms, touching up my makeup, the other girls were studying men. When I was going onstage and traveling, see, a lot of the best ones got scooped up."

In a white limousine, Aretha led the way for Jones to visit her house, taking him past huge, well-tended houses and lawns, "down a tree-shaded dirt lane to a stark white six-bedroom house where an Excalibur with the license plate ZOOMIN waits in the drive." She showed off the rosebushes she had planted. A small dog barked and wagged its tail on her porch. She said she lived with her family, though not her sons, and Jones didn't mention seeing anyone around. Occasionally she went to movies with friends and neighbors.

Aretha and Jones discussed the biographical movie about singing star Tina Turner's career and violent marriage. Aretha said the story bore no resemblance to her own. When Jones asked her whom she would like to play in a movie about her own life, Aretha replied "sarcastically," as Jones described her tone: "Natalie Cole maybe." But Aretha didn't seem at all threatened by Natalie Cole.

Aretha could recall in detail, however, the problems she faced about thirty years earlier when she had been booked to go on the *Ed Sullivan Show*. "They said my gown was too low-cut. . .I don't think it was. . . . It was a beautifully beaded gown, but I don't think that at that time they had seen a black woman on network TV showing so much cleavage. . . . I had several other, high-cut gowns that we went to, but there were so many artists on that evening that I got cut. . .I was worn out. . .I had rehearsed a long time for that appearance. . .I just went out the back door crying."[27]

"Suddenly I remember Liz Smith's little scolding in the paper, and I realize why Miss Franklin is so sensitive about her wardrobe," wrote Jones. "And I leave her in the house with the rhinestone crown and her photos of her father, still looking for what's real."

In Detroit, the big yellow brick house where her father lived, and in which she grew up with her brothers and sisters, still stood unoccupied. She went near it sometimes, when she shopped for groceries. She could not bring herself to sell it, for her roots were her comfort and her sorrow, her weakness and her strength.

On December 4, 1994, Aretha received the Kennedy Center Honors Award for 1993, for her lifetime contribution to the performing arts. Aretha sang along with the new Bethel Baptist Church choir in Washington, D.C., for the occasion.

Pianist Teddy Harris, who still lived in Detroit and was in touch with her occasionally, thought that she was happier than she had been earlier in her life, because her career had risen above all obstacles and brought her such satisfaction and respect. "She must have a piano in every room of her house," he said. "Music helped her survive all her problems."[28]

SOURCE NOTES

CHAPTER ONE

1. Mark Bego, *Aretha Franklin: The Queen of Soul* (New York: St. Martin's Press, 1989), p. 16.
2. Author's personal interview with Joe Sundiard of the *Detroit Free Press.*
3. *Time*, "Lady Soul: Singing It Like It Is," June 28, 1968, pp. 62–65.
4. Ibid.
5. Leslie Gourse, *Louis' Children* (New York: William Morrow, 1984), p. 18.
6. James T. Jones IV, "Soul of the Queen," *Vanity Fair* (March 1994) pp. 56–73.
7. Ibid.
8. Jerry Wexler and David Ritz, *Rhythm and the Blues* (New York: Alfred A. Knopf, 1993), [n.p.].
9. *Time*, June 28, 1968.
10. From "Aretha Franklin: The Queen of Soul," broadcast on PBS's *American Masters* series, 1988.

CHAPTER TWO

1. James T. Jones IV, "Soul of the Queen." *Vanity Fair* (March 1994) pp. 56–73.

2. *Time*, June 28, 1968.
3. Jones.
4. *Time*, June 28, 1968.
5. Jones.
6. *Ibid.*
7. Mark Bego, *Aretha Franklin: The Queen of Soul* (New York: St. Martin's Press, 1989), p. 17.
8. Bego, p. 17.
9. *Ibid.*
10. Bego; "Aretha Franklin: The Queen of Soul," broadcast on PBS's *American Masters* series, 1988.
11. "Aretha Franklin: The Queen of Soul," broadcast on PBS's *American Masters* series, 1988.
12. Bego, p. 27.
13. Jerry Wexler, in a personal interview with the author, n.d.
14. *Ibid.*

CHAPTER THREE
1. "Aretha Franklin: The Queen of Soul," broadcast on PBS's *American Masters* series, 1988.
2. Cecil Franklin, as interviewed in video, "Aretha Franklin: The Queen of Soul," 1988.
3. Aretha Franklin, as interviewed in video, "Aretha Franklin: The Queen of Soul," 1988.
4. John Hammond, as interviewed in video, "Aretha Franklin: The Queen of Soul," 1988.
5. Drummer Ray Brooks, in a personal interview with the author, n.d.
6. Ted Fox, *Showtime at the Apollo* (New York: Holt, Rinehart, Winston, 1983), p. 266.
7. Leonard Feather, "Evil Gal Blues," *Modern Age Music.*
8. *Village Voice*, n.d.
9. *Ibid.*
10. Jerry Wexler, in a personal interview with the author, n.d.

11. *Time*, June, 28, 1968.
12. James T. Jones IV, "Soul of the Queen." *Vanity Fair* (March 1994) pp. 56–73.
13. Teddy Harris and Roy Brooks, in personal interviews with the author, n.d.
14. Teddy Harris, in a personal interview with the author, n.d.
15. Jerry Wexler, in a personal interview with the author, n.d.
16. Clyde Otis, as interviewed in "Aretha Franklin: The Queen of Soul," broadcast on PBS's *American Masters* series, 1988.
17. Jones, pp. 56–73.

CHAPTER FOUR

1. "Aretha Franklin: The Queen of Soul," broadcast on PBS's *American Masters* series, 1988.
2. Jerry Wexler and David Ritz, *Rhythm and the Blues* (New York: Alfred A. Knopf, 1993), [n.p.]; Jerry Wexler, in a personal interview with the author, n.d.
3. "Aretha Franklin: The Queen of Soul," broadcast on PBS's *American Masters* series, 1988.
4. Wexler and Ritz, p. 204.
5. Herman Wright, in a personal interview with the author, n.d.
6. Jerry Wexler, in a personal interview with the author, n.d.
7. Wexler, personal interview, n.d.
8. Wexler, personal interview, n.d.; Wexler and Ritz, p. 208.
9. Wexler, personal interview, n.d.; Wexler and Ritz, p. 210.
10. "Aretha Franklin: The Queen of Soul," broadcast on PBS's *American Masters* series, 1988.
11. *Ibid.*
12. *Ibid.*
13. Wexler and Ritz, p. 212.

14. "Aretha Franklin: The Queen of Soul," broadcast on PBS's *American Masters* series, 1988.

CHAPTER FIVE

1. "Aretha Franklin: The Queen of Soul," broadcast on PBS's *American Masters* series, 1988.
2. Nikki Giovanni, "Poem for Aretha," *New York Live*, June 20, 1993.
3. John S. Wilson, *The New York Times*, September 30, 1967.
4. Tom Phillips, *The New York Times*, October 28, 1967.
5. Jack Robbins, *New York Post*, October 28, 1967.
6. "Aretha Franklin: The Queen of Soul," broadcast on PBS's *American Masters* series, 1988.
7. Jerry Wexler, as interviewed in "Aretha Franklin: The Queen of Soul," broadcast on PBS's *American Masters* series, 1988.
8. Mark Bego, *Aretha Franklin: The Queen of Soul* (New York: St. Martin's Press, 1989), p. 108.
9. Burt Korall, *Saturday Review*, March 16, 1968.
10. Robert Shelton, *The New York Times*, June 29, 1968.
11. Gerry Goffin and Carole King, "(You Make Me Feel) Like a Natural Woman," Columbia-Screen Gems, BMI, n.d.
12. *Time*, "Lady Soul: Singing It Like It Is," June 28, 1968, pp. 62–65.
13. Anthony Heilbut, *The Gospel Sound* (New York: Limelight Editions, 1982), p. xxv.
14. *Time*, June 28, 1968.
15. *Ibid.*
16. James T. Jones IV, "Soul of the Queen." *Vanity Fair* (March 1994) pp. 56–73.
17. Donald Walden, in a personal interview with the author, n.d.
18. Bego, p. 95.
19. Walden, personal interview, n.d.

20. Robert Shelton, *The New York Times*, October, 14, 1968.
21. Walden, personal interview, n.d.
22. *Ibid.*
23. *Ibid.*
24. *Ibid.*
25. *Ibid.*
26. Bego, p. 77.
27. *Ibid.*, p. 91
28. *Ibid.*, p. 91
29. *Ibid.*, p. 93
30. Peter Guralnick, *Sweet Soul Music: Rhythm and Blues and the Southern Dream of Freedom* (New York: HarperCollins, 1986), n.p.
31. Jerry Wexler, in a personal interview with the author, n.d.

CHAPTER SIX

1. James T. Jones IV, "Soul of the Queen." *Vanity Fair* (March 1994) pp. 56–73.
2. *Ibid.*
3. David N. Bromberg, *Village Voice*, February 5, 1970.
4. *Amsterdam News*, July 4, 1970.
5. *Jet*, November 12, 1970.
6. *Ibid.*
7. Clayton Riley, *The New York Times*, November 1, 1970.
8. C. Gerald Fraser, *The New York Times*, November 1, 1970.
9. *Ibid.*
10. *Jet*, November 12, 1970.
11. "Aretha Franklin: The Queen of Soul," broadcast on PBS's *American Masters* series, 1988.

CHAPTER SEVEN

1. Mark Bego, *Aretha Franklin: The Queen of Soul* (New York: St. Martin's Press, 1989), p. 161.
2. *Ibid.*, pp. 162–163.

3. Anthony Heilbut, *The Gospel Sound* (New York: Limelight Editions, 1982), p. 306.
4. "Aretha Franklin: The Queen of Soul," broadcast on PBS's *American Masters* series, 1988.
5. *Ibid.*
6. Bego, p. 173.
7. Robert Palmer, *The New York Times*, March 1978.

CHAPTER EIGHT

1. Robert Palmer, *The New York Times*, January 1981.
2. George Kanzler, *Newark Star Ledger*, September 6, 1981.
3. David Hinckley, *New York Daily News*, November 1982.
4. Joe Black, *New York Daily News*, November 1, 1982.
5. Maurice Prince, owner of Snack 'n' Chat restaurant, in personal interview with author, n.d.

CHAPTER NINE

1. Mark Bego, *Aretha Franklin: The Queen of Soul* (New York: St. Martin's Press, 1989), p. 221.
2. "Aretha Franklin: The Queen of Soul," broadcast on PBS's *American Masters* series, 1988.
3. Bego, p. 221.
4. *Ibid.*, p. 222.
5. *Ibid.*, p. 226.
6. "Aretha Franklin: The Queen of Soul," broadcast on PBS's *American Masters* series, 1988.
7. Bego, p. 240.
8. *Ibid.*, p. 243.

CHAPTER TEN

1. Mark Bego, *Aretha Franklin: The Queen of Soul* (New York: St. Martin's Press, 1989), p. 277.

2. Homer Bigart, *The New York Times*, March 14, 1968.
3. *Time*, "Lady Soul: Singing It Like It Is," June 28, 1968, pp. 62–65.
4. Jon Pareles, *The New York Times*, August 22, 1988.
5. James T. Jones IV, "Soul of the Queen." *Vanity Fair* (March 1994) pp. 56–73.
6. David Hinckley, *New York Daily News*, 1989.
7. Jon Pareles, *The New York Times*, July 8, 1989.
8. *Ibid.*
9. Ira Robbins, *New York Post*, July 7, 1989.
10. David Hinckley, *New York Daily News*, July 7, 1989.
11. Jones.
12. Jon Pareles, *The New York Times*, July 8, 1989.
13. Stephen Holden, *The New York Times*, September 1991.
14. Gary Giddins, *Village Voice*, October 13, 1992.
15. *New York Post*, November 25, 1992.
16. *Ibid.*
17. *New York Post*, December 30, 1992.
18. Aretha Franklin, in personal interview with the author, n.d.
19. Jon Pareles, *The New York Times*, April 29, 1993.
20. Sheila Rule, *The New York Times*, April 24, 1993.
21. Aretha Franklin, in personal conversation with the author, n.d.
22. Jones.
23. *Ibid.*
24. *Ibid.*
25. *Ibid.*
26. *Ibid.*
27. *Ibid.*
28. Teddy Harris, in personal interview with the author, n.d.

SUGGESTED LISTENING AND VIEWING

SOUL, INCLUDING POP, RHYTHM AND BLUES, JAZZ, AND ROCK

Aretha Franklin: Jazz To Soul, New York: Columbia/ Legacy, Sony Music Entertainment, Inc., 1992.

Songs included are: "Today I Sing the Blues," "Blue by Myself," "Maybe I'm a Fool," "All Night Long," "Blue Holiday," "Nobody Like You," "Sweet Lover," "Just for a Thrill," "If Ever I Would Leave You," "Once in a While," "This Bitter Earth," "God Bless the Child," "Skylark," "Muddy Water," "Drinking Again," "What a Difference a Day Makes," "Unforgettable," "Love for Sale," "Misty," "Impossible," "This Could Be the Start of Something," "Won't Be Long," "Operation Heartbreak," "Soulville," "Runnin' Out of Fools," "Trouble in Mind," "Walk On By" "Every Little Bit Hurts," "Mockingbird," "You'll Lose a Good Thing," "Cry Like a Baby," "Take It Like You Give It," "Land of Dreams," "Can't You Just See Me," "(No No,) I'm Losing You," "Bit of Soul," "Why Was I Born?," "Until You Were Gone," "Lee Cross."

Aretha Franklin: 30 Greatest Hits, New York: Atlantic Recording Company, 1986.

Songs included are: "I Never Loved a Man (The Way I Love You)," "Respect," "Do Right Woman, Do Right Man," "Dr. Feelgood," "Save Me," "Baby I Love You," "You Make Me Feel Like a Natural Woman," "Chain of Fools," "Since You've Been Gone," "Ain't No Way," "Think," "I Say a Little Prayer," "The House That Jack Built," "See Saw," "The Weight," "Share Your Love With Me," "Eleanor Rigby," "Call Me," "Spirit in the Dark," "Don't Play That Song," "You're All I Need to Get By," "Bridge Over Troubled Water," "Spanish Harlem," "Rock Steady," "Oh Me Oh My, I'm a Fool for You Baby," "Day Dreaming," "Wholly Holy," "Angel," "Until You Come Back to Me," "I'm in Love."

Aretha Franklin: Greatest Hits, 1980-1994, New York: Arista Records, Inc., 1994.

Songs included are: "Freeway of Love," "I Knew You Were Waiting (For Me)," "Jump to It," "Willing to Forgive," "Doctor's Orders," "United Together," "Who's Zoomin' Who?," "A Deeper Love," "Honey," "Get It Right," "Another Night," "Ever Changing *Times,*" "Jimmy Lee," "You Make Me Feel (Like a Natural Woman)," "I Dreamed a Dream."

GOSPEL

Amazing Grace, New York: Atlantic Recording Company, 1972.

(Many of her original LPs are available in second-hand record stores, such as Footlights, on East 12th Street between Third and Fourth Avenues in New York City. Much of her music has also been reissued on compact discs.)

154

BIBLIOGRAPHY

Bego, Mark. *Aretha Franklin, The Queen of Soul.* New York: St. Martin's Press, 1989.

Brooks, Tilford. *American Black Musical Heritage.* Englewood Cliffs, N.J.: Prentice-Hall, Inc., 1984.

Ellison, Mary. *Extensions of the Blues.* London: John Calder Ltd., 1989.

Feather, Leonard, and Ira Gitler. *The Encyclopedia of Jazz in the Seventies.* New York: Horizon Press, 1976.

Fox, Ted. *Showtime at the Apollo.* New York: Holt, Rinehart and Winston, 1983.

Gourse, Leslie. *Louis' Children.* New York: Quill Books, 1984.

Guralnick, Peter. *Sweet Soul Music.* New York: Harper & Row, 1986.

Jones, LeRoi. *Blues People.* New York: William Morrow Co., Inc., 1963.

Harris, Michael W. *The Rise of Gospel Blues.* New York: Oxford University Press, 1992.

Pruter, Robert, ed. *The Blackwell Guide to Soul Recordings.* Oxford: Basil Blackwell Ltd, 1993.

Schwerin, Jules. *Got to Tell It: Mahalia Jackson, Queen of Gospel.* New York: Oxford University Press, 1992.

Wexler, Jerry, and David Ritz. *Rhythm and the Blues.* New York: Alfred A. Knopf, 1993.

VIDEOGRAPHY

"Aretha Franklin: The Queen of Soul," produced for Public Broadcasting System by WNET, New York, 1988. "Aretha Franklin: Live at Park West," Rhino Home Video, 1992.

INDEX